John Henry Wigmore

The Australian Ballot System

As embodied in the legislation of various countries

John Henry Wigmore

The Australian Ballot System
As embodied in the legislation of various countries

ISBN/EAN: 9783337314828

Printed in Europe, USA, Canada, Australia, Japan

Cover: Foto ©Suzi / pixelio.de

More available books at **www.hansebooks.com**

THE

AUSTRALIAN BALLOT SYSTEM

AS

EMBODIED IN THE LEGISLATION OF
VARIOUS COUNTRIES.

WITH AN HISTORICAL INTRODUCTION.

By JOHN H. WIGMORE,
OF THE BOSTON BAR.

BOSTON:
CHARLES C. SOULE.
1889.

Copyright, 1889,
BY JOHN H. WIGMORE.

UNIVERSITY PRESS:
JOHN WILSON AND SON, CAMBRIDGE.

PREFACE.

WORKERS in the field of foreign statutory law must in this country frequently be at a loss for complete materials of recent date; and in preparing the following pages the editor has not been able to consult the statutes of New Zealand since 1883, or of Tasmania and Western Australia since 1884, or to obtain complete information as to legislation in Victoria or New South Wales since 1885, or in several European countries since 1886. These deficiencies are to some extent unavoidable in an American work. No complete set of Australian reports and statutes exists in this country. *Pasinomie* is not to be procured in Boston, probably not in the United States. The *Annuaire de législation étrangère*, published by the *Société de législation comparée*, does not appear until twelve months or more after the year with which it deals (the volume for 1886 has only recently reached this country); and the *Bulletin* published by the same society, though its reports are as recent as can reasonably be expected, has by no means the exhaustive character of the *Annuaire*. To prepare a complete notice of foriegn legislation to date is perhaps not possible, in the nature of the case, in any country.

It is believed, however, that the only changes, if any, that are likely to have occurred are the possible adoption of the Australian system in other European States, and a revision of the Tasmanian statutes, which have served since 1858.

PREFACE.

The side notes to the statutes are collateral references to the other statutes given in full, and are intended to include the principal provisions as to which there is a variation in the practice of different states. The numbered notes at the end of the Massachusetts statute are comments on the comparative advantages of the different variations. Where two or more statutes of a single country are given, they are referred to in the notes as A, B, etc., according to their order in the text.

The Queensland and South Australian statutes were selected from the seven Australasian laws for these reasons: The seven statutes, as will be seen, fall into two general classes, those of S. Australia and W. Australia being substantially the same, and those of Victoria, Queensland and the remaining states being not materially unlike. The S. Australian statute, as being the most important of its class, and that of Queensland, as having received later revision than the others of its class, are given in full, and the variations of the remaining Australian statutes in all important details are noted in Part VIII.

Those who are concerned in advancing legislation on the subject are requested to send to the editor, as soon as may be, 1. a copy of the draft of any bill, as soon as introduced; 2. a copy of any law, as soon as enacted and approved; together with any additional information relative to the history of the movement on behalf of ballot reform. It will thus be made possible, in a subsequent edition of the book, not only to record whatever new legislation takes place upon the subject, but also to make known to other States whatever desirable improvements of detail may elsewhere have been devised, even though they have failed to be enacted.

J. H. W.

BOSTON, Jan. 21, 1889.

CONTENTS.

	PAGE
PREFACE	iii
INTRODUCTORY SKETCH OF THE HISTORY OF THE AUSTRALIAN BALLOT SYSTEM	1

STATUTES:

PART I. MASSACHUSETTS	37
NOTES ON PARALLEL PROVISIONS (OF THE VARIOUS ACTS) RELATING TO THE SAME SUBJECT	52
PART II. SOUTH AUSTRALIA	68
PART III. QUEENSLAND	75
PART IV. GREAT BRITAIN AND IRELAND . . .	85
PART V. BELGIUM	105
PART VI. KENTUCKY	116
PART VII. NEW YORK	122
PART VIII. SUMMARY OF STATUTES IN OTHER COUNTRIES: —	
A. TASMANIA	133
B. NEW ZEALAND	134
C. VICTORIA	135
D. NEW SOUTH WALES	135
E. WEST AUSTRALIA	136
F. DOMINION OF CANADA	137
G. QUEBEC	140

PART VIII. SUMMARY OF STATUTES (*continued*) . . PAGE
    H. ONTARIO 143
    I. WISCONSIN 145
    J. LUXEMBOURG 146
    K. ITALY 147
    L. NORWAY 148
    M. AUSTRIA 149
    N. OTHER COUNTRIES 149

APPENDIX 153

INTRODUCTION.

WHERE a community has reason to believe itself to be numbered among the enlightened ones of its age, and its institutions to be pre-eminent among those of civilized mankind as types of liberty and progress, it relaxes (it may be) the constant strain of high endeavor; an easy complacency settles upon it; and it awakes one day to realize that a community having no pretensions to as conspicuous a rank among nations has grasped the torch of progress, and now leads the way with intelligent and advanced methods, pointing the path for its more eminent fellows to pursue.

With some such reflection as this must England and our own commonwealths look upon the history of ballot reform in the past fifty years. Before representative government in Australasia had an existence, corruption, fraud, and intimidation (to name none of the less palpable evils that beset an election) thrived abundantly in Great Britain and Ireland, and even in our own country had begun to take root. But it was reserved for stripling states, when to them in their turn the exigency came, not merely to apply, but to invent an effective remedy, and to indicate a cure for at any rate the grosser evils that prevent an election from being what at the least it should be, the free and accurate expression of the opinions of the electors. It is proposed in the following introductory pages to sketch the history of the measure known as the Australian ballot system, as it passed from state to state in Australasia, on to the mother country in Europe, thence westward to Canada and eastward to continental countries, and finally westward again to these United States; and in conclusion to take up, briefly, the reasons underlying its effectiveness, and the application of its principles to political conditions in this country.

I.

That the system is by birth Australian has once, and once only, been questioned. In 1869, when the British Parliamentary Committee were considering the introduction of the secret ballot, and were examining witnesses from all parts of the world, it was told[1] that in the little town of Maryport, in Cumberland, a similar method of voting had for many years been in successful operation, and it was the grievance of the burgesses of the old town that Australia, far from deserving the credit of an invention, had been only a borrower, without acknowledgment, of the Maryport method, doubtless carried to the colonies by some native of the town.[2] Whether the method used in

[1] Testimony of Francis Taylor, Report of Com. on Parl. and Mun. Elections. Parl. Papers, 1868-9, vol. viii. p. 525.

[2] That a town of Maryport appears on the map of Queensland perhaps adds to the plausibility of this claim.

Maryport was in fact a similar one, and whether it antedated the colonial system, may be dismissed from our consideration; for there can be little doubt that the latter was purely indigenous, that its details were prepared and marked out independently, and that no other system was searched for, referred to, or known by the framers of the law. This we have upon the authority of the father of the measure, Francis S. Dutton, member of the Legislature of South Australia from 1851 to 1865, and during that time twice at the head of the government. The secret ballot was first proposed by him in the session of Legislative Council of 1851, before representative government and universal suffrage had been granted to South Australia.[1] At that time the usual attendant vices of open elections already flourished in the young colony. Rioting and violence, bribery, intimidation, and coercion, were only too common, — even more so, some said, than in England. But for several years no action was effected in the direction of reform. In 1856 came the Constitution, granting popular representation and manhood suffrage. From 1857 to 1859 Dutton was a member of the government, and immediately used the opportunity to advance his favorite measure. No commission of inquiry was appointed, but with the aid of Chief-Justice (then Attorney-General) Hanson, the details of a plan were elaborated and a bill introduced which, after receiving modifications and additions in the House, became a law under the name of the Elections Act, 1857–8 (No. 12), and

[1] Parl. Papers, *supra*, p. 353.

typifies the system which has since spread to two other continents. "I can safely say," said Dutton, many years later, standing before the Marquis of Hartington's committee, "that no act of my political life has given me so much satisfaction as what I did fifteen or sixteen years ago with reference to the ballot system. If that is possible, I am more strongly in favor of it now, after fifteen years' experience, than when I introduced it before I had any experience about it." It so happened that Colonel (since Sir) Robert Richard Torrens (then recently the author of a system of registration of land titles which has earned him an international reputation and has stimulated Canada and Great Britain to efforts in the same direction) was at that time also a member of the Government, and, imbued with the arguments of Lord Palmerston and John Stuart Mill, had strenuously opposed the introduction of the secret ballot. That its results completely converted him we learn from his own confession. He came to believe that the system he had opposed was "the best and most rapid and facile mode of carrying on elections." The new machinery worked with "the greatest smoothness, ease, and economy." We have his testimony that the aspect of elections was completely changed. Rioting and disorder disappeared entirely. The day of polling saw such quietness that a stranger would not realize that an election was going on. Intimidation by landlords and dictation by trades unions alike ceased. Canvassing, at least upon an organized plan, was practically given up. Perhaps Mr. Dutton's most significant statement (and yet the one most difficult for us to picture) is that the very notion of exercising coercion or improper influence "absolutely died out of the country." The united sentiment of the colony accorded with these views, and has ever since sustained without dissent the policy of the act. By the Ballot Act of 1862 (25 Vict., No. 13) its principles were applied to all elections to public bodies other than the Legislative Council and the Assembly, and thus became applicable from time to time in municipal elections; and by the District Councils Act of 1876 (39 Vict., No. 43) and the more recent one of 1887 (50 Vict. No. 41), the system was applied to rural government also. The statute governing legislative elections has from time to time been revised (Elections Act, 1861, No. 20; Elections Act, 1870, No. 18; Elections Act, 1879, No. 141), usually with reference to the suffrage qualification and the registration of electors; and the ballot system of thirty years ago now extends to all elections alike — municipal, rural, and legislative — in the colony.

In Victoria an almost simultaneous movement took place in favor of the secret ballot. The project was introduced by Mr. William Nicholson, and the ministerial opposition to it speedily resulted in a change of government. Nicholson, at first unsuccessful in forming a ministry, afterwards became Chief Secretary, and at the head of the government carried through the measure in 1856, two years after the Constitution had created a representative legislature. The opposition to the secret ballot came mainly from the Conservatives (as was the case later in England), and from a few prominent Liberals; but after its working in practice was seen, the Conservatives were thoroughly converted, and the country as a unit declared in its favor. Bribery and corruption seem never to have existed in Victoria to such an extent as in neighboring South Australia. But other evils politic were not wanting. The new system secured quietness and convenience, and abolished the tumult and wild disorder which formerly prevailed. The various phases of intimidation disappeared;[1] and a personal canvass, that formerly indispensable feature of a British election, became almost an unknown occurrence.[2] Electioneering is largely confined to holding public meetings, at which the merits of candidates and of measures are discussed. About 1861 the operation of the secret-ballot system was extended to other than parliamentary elections by the Local Government Act (No. 176). In 1869, upon the reorganization of county and municipal government, it was re-enacted by the Shires Act (No. 358) and the Boroughs Statute (No. 359); and was perpetuated, when these provisions were again fused into one statute, in the Local Government Act, 1874 (No. 506). As applied to parliamentary elections, it is now con-

---

[1] For instance, "The ballot has saved many a man from having his mortgage foreclosed upon him, as was the case under the old system." — *Melbourne Gazette*, 1856, quoted in "*Facts about the Ballot*," published by the Ballot Society, London, 1857.

[2] This is corroborated by the statement of Mr. Nicholson in "*Facts about the Ballot*," supra. See this pamphlet for a full account of the adoption and success of the system in Victoria.

tained in the Electoral Act of 1865 (No. 279). During nearly thirty years of the operation of the system, only sixteen decisions of the Supreme Court were asked for the construction of the acts containing it.[1]

The new system spread rapidly in the land of its birth. It was adopted in Tasmania Feb. 25, 1858, by the Parliamentary Elections Act (21 Vict., No. 32), which has ever since served without revision; and in 1865 the Rural Municipalities Act (29 Vict., No. 8) extended the method to elections other than parliamentary. In the same year, 1858, New South Wales entered the ranks, and applied the new system to its parliamentary elections (22 Vict., No. 20). Subsequent statutes embodying the subject are the Municipalities Act, 1867 (31 Vict., No. 12), and the Elections Act, 1880 (44 Vict., No. 13). New Zealand apparently did not adopt the new method in its essence until 1870; for although a "Regulation of Elections Act" was passed, bearing date August 19, 1858, by which only the officers of election and persons actually voting were admitted to the polling-places, yet the voter was still required, as in England, to declare verbally to the polling-clerk the name of the desired candidate, and no attempt was made to require secrecy of those present at the time. We must therefore say that not until the Regulation of Elections Act, 1870 (33–34 Vict., No. 18), was ballot reform adopted in New Zealand. Under the

[1] No decisions since 1883 are accessible to the editor. The above statement is of course made of those provisions only which form a part of the electoral machinery peculiar to the ballot system, and not of those parts of the acts relating to registration, etc.

Revising Act of 1881 (45 Vict., No. 12), and the Municipal Corporations Act of 1876,[1] it is believed that the secret ballot system is in vogue at all elections in New Zealand. In Queensland (which did not receive responsible government until 1859), and in West Australia (which still continues a crown colony), the exact date of the introduction of the system cannot be stated. In the Queensland Parliamentary Elections Act, 1874, appear in substance the same regulations afterwards re-enacted in the Parliamentary Elections Act of 1885 (given in Part III., *infra*). By the Local Government Act 1878 (42 Vict., No. 8), these principles were applied to municipal elections, and by the recent Divisional Boards Act of 1887 (51 Vict., No. 7) their operation has been extended to the choice of what correspond to county officers; so that all elections are now conducted according to this system. In Western Australia, legislative elections are now held under the Ballot Act of 1877 (41 Vict., No. 15), based on the Elections Act of South Australia and embodying its essential principles. Whether in the Election Act of 1870 (33 Vict., No. 13) similar provisions already existed, the editor has not been able to ascertain.[2]

[1] This the editor has not been able to consult.

[2] A few words of contemporary testimony as to the working of the system in Australia may be of interest. They are taken from an interview published in the "Boston Herald" of Dec. 29, 1888, with a prominent Australian then stopping in Boston.

"It has been said that the new system will lead to confusion and delay at the polls. Has this been the case in Australia?" was the first question.

" Not at all. . . . Very little work is done near the polls in the in-

Meanwhile, the good results of the Australian system of voting had reached England, where thoughtful men were anxiously looking for some solution of the problem of pure and tranquil elections. The earliest method of choosing members of the lower

terests of the several candidates; it may be said none at all. The campaign is conducted much the same as in the States, by means of meetings, pamphlets, and flyers. Work at the polls is impossible, and it does not pay to work at the distance prescribed by law."

... "Is the system of voting now in use generally accepted as satisfactory and regarded as permanent in Australia."

"Yes; I think so. I have never known any serious opposition, nor of any attempt to essentially modify it."

... "In regard to the nominations, all who desire to be candidates offer themselves as such. This does not lead, as might be supposed, to a multiplicity of candidates and a disastrous splitting of the party vote. The Australian is a pretty sensible fellow, and does not encourage candidates who have no chance. Before the day of election, the contest is usually narrowed down to two candidates for each office."

The speaker illustrated the true freedom of voting attained under the system by citing facts coming under his knowledge in England.

"The reform was pushed most vigorously by the Radicals, who expected large gains in voting strength from the increased privacy afforded by the new method. . . . The new ballot law did prevent this undue influence by the employing classes, but it also made impossible bull-dozing and terrorism by caucuses and committees. The result of this twofold influence was different from that expected by the Radical leaders. Under the protection afforded by the absolute secrecy of the ballot, more voted against them than for them. The voters attend the Radical meetings and shout themselves hoarse; but when the day of election arrives they go to the polls and, unknown to the Radical committees, vote for the Conservative candidates. This explains why some districts in England, in which it is impossible to hold a Conservative meeting without a row, return that party's nominees by large majorities. Rather than be ostracized and maltreated by their comrades, many of the workingmen join hands with the Radicals before the election, but vote as they choose at the polling-booths, and they very often choose to stand with the more conservative elements of society."

House, — used at a time when, as is probable, all the freemen of the shire had a voice in the selection, — was by the view or show of hands, usually in an open, unenclosed space, or by some similar rough process.[1] Not until after a statute of 8 Henry VI. (1429), restricting the county suffrage to 40-shilling freeholders, do we hear of a poll being taken. As late as the sixteenth century the show of hands was still regarded as sufficient in law, and, though gradually a change was insisted upon, not before the statute of 7 & 8 Wm. III. c. 125 (1696) was the right to demand a poll finally established. In other respects, also, the antiquated methods were only slowly adapted to modern needs. An election frequently lasted eight or nine days. In one instance early in this century the polls were open in Mayo County for fifty-seven days; though later laws limited the duration of a poll to two days in the country and one day in the boroughs. The usual process was this: The voter entered the polling-booth, gave his name to the poll-clerk, and, if successful in replying as to his qualifications, was required to declare aloud for whom he voted, and the clerk checked a vote for that candidate opposite his name in the poll-book. The poll was technically only an adjournment of the elections, which began with what was in fact the nomination of candidates in open meeting. If a poll was demanded, which happened as a matter of course when more than one candidate appeared, the election was declared adjourned, and the poll took place at the ad-

---

[1] Cox, Antient Parliamentary Elections, p. 105.

journment.[1] By the first half of this century (and matters became worse as each decade passed) serious abuses had fastened themselves upon this system. The development of industrial and social conditions, the increase of popular influence, the gradual shifting of political contests from the battlefield and the court to Parliament and the polls, — these causes, with others, resulted in placing an inordinate strain upon the outgrown methods. Ever since its first days, indeed, in the time of Henry VI., the open poll had shown its failings. One is half amused to read the ingenuous complaint presented in 1451 by certain freemen of Huntingdonshire, protesting against the election of two knights returned for the shire, and telling a tale of armed opponents, who threatened violence at the polls, "and soe wee departed for dread of the inconveniences that was likely to be done for manslaughter." Other documents of the times suggest to us that even the credit of having originated "counting out" methods and falsification of returns, with other characteristic practices, may upon investigation be taken from the American ward politician; for in a preamble to the statute of 23 Henry VI. c. 14 it is regretfully recited that "divers sheriffs of the counties of the realm of England, for their singular avail and lucre, have not made due elec-

---

[1] Before the reform of 1872 the practice had been adopted in certain boroughs of voting by delivering to the poll-clerk voting-papers signed by the elector and containing the name of the preferred candidate. The varying procedure was reducible substantially to these two types.

tions;"[1] and this passage is not without its companion instances. From this time on, but more abundantly as our own century was reached, violence, corruption, fraud, and intimidation in all its phases and varieties were frequent, — in one place or at one time more or less noticeable than at another place or time, but always increasing, and, especially in the larger cities and their environs,[2] resulting finally in a condition of affairs which was described by high authority as "frightful." One of the commonest facts of British elections, before 1872, was the controlling influence exercised by large customers over tradesmen of all sorts. Landlords intimidated their tenants, and marched detachments to the polls to vote in their interests. In one place employers coerced their workmen; and in another the trades unions coerced their members. Worse than all, and hardly to be believed, in larger cities hired mobs often patrolled the streets, keeping away hostile voters and intimidating those who ventured to the polls. A Conservative mob or a Radical or Liberal mob, or both, were in some places a common feature of an election. On one occasion which may serve as an example, some 500 out of 2,000 Conservative voters were prevented by demonstrations of violence from giving their votes. Just as present political methods in our large cities should not be taken as

[1] This word here signifies the ministerial act of certifying to the result of the election.

[2] See the testimony before the Bribery at Elections Committee, Parl. Papers, 1835, vol. viii.

types of political conduct in every part of the republic, so these instances are not to be regarded as representing the condition of things throughout Great Britain. But that they could exist at all under the British electoral system was reason enough for a reform. From time to time the secret ballot had been demanded by men of influence as a possible remedy. James Mill and the Benthamites, Peel, O'Connell, Bright, Lord Russell, Grote, Macaulay, — all these names are associated with the efforts of the first half of the century.[1] But secret voting has in England always had to encounter a special argument of predominant influence. It is difficult to sum it up in a few words, but its burden is that the open vote tends to create and maintain the self-respect of the voter, and that the secret vote is the parent of hypocrisy. The strength of this sentiment

---

[1] The following passage-at-arms will serve to show the vigor with which the movement was carried on in controversial literature: —

"Objection 26: That Publicity is the main essence of the representative system. Ans. Is the elector's being kicked the main essence of the representative system? Is the elector's being bribed the main essence of the representative system? If they are, the publicity which secures them may be so too. Some people think that if the voter has a right to vote, he has a right to vote without being kicked. Some people think that if he is to choose a legislator for the public, it is good he should do it with as little chance of bribery as may be. Some even go to the length of thinking these are of the main essence. Will anybody tell us how the voter is to do better for being either kicked or bribed? But it is good that the voter should go through great tribulation. In the Life of Alexander by Quintus Curtius is the story of a man who, after giving his evidence to the best of his ability, was put to the torture, to see if he 'would say the same under torment.' In like manner, with the voter it is held necessary to see whether he will vote the same under torment." (From *Fallacies against the Ballot, with the Answers:* published by the Ballot Society, 1855.)

among many of the more thoughtful men in England is something which perhaps has not been appreciated in this country.[1] We may conceive that to enact compulsory secrecy in voting will to some conservative Americans perhaps appear a step too far; but the denial of even an optional secrecy such as we now enjoy is a policy which to many of us would be almost incomprehensible.

In the elections of 1868, however, matters reached a climax, and the month of March, 1869, saw a committee appointed, with the Marquis of Hartington in the chair, to inquire into the existing methods of conducting elections, in order to provide further guarantees for the "tranquillity, purity, and freedom" of parliamentary and municipal elections.[2] The committee held sessions during three months, unearthed various accounts of corruption and intimidation at the previous elections, and examined witnesses from Australia, the United States, France, Italy, and Greece, steadily endeavoring to secure some comprehensive solution of the problem. They reported, in July, 1869, only the evidence taken before them, but upon reappointment, in the session

---

[1] See an article by James Mill, in 18 Westminster Rev. 1. See also Edinb. Rev. 1853, pp. 572, 610. This feeling still lingers here and there in England with all the vitality of a traditional sentiment, and it was probably to its influence that the seven years' limitation of the original Ballot Act was due. See 115 Westm. Rev. 443 (1881). Indeed no stronger evidence is needed of the merits of the act than the fact that the secret ballot is not in accord with the traditions of British politics, and is retained in the British electoral system purely for the immense benefits which it is seen to secure.

[2] Parl. Papers, 1868-1869, vol. viii.; 1870, vol. vi.

of 1870, they reported a recommendation that the secret ballot be adopted. The fruit of the movement was the Ballot Act of 1872, brought in on Feb. 20, 1870, by William E. Forster, Secretary Bruce, and Lord Hartington, and recommitted and amended from session to session for more than two years, until on May 30, 1872, it passed the Commons, and subsequently took its place among the statutes as 35 & 36 Vict., c. 33, — based substantially on the South Australian method, but modified, enlarged, and carefully applied to the circumstances of its new home. Fortunately we are not without testimony as to its operation. Four years later, on the motion of Sir Charles Dilke, a committee was appointed, with that noted Liberal as chairman, "to inquire into the working of the machinery of the Ballot Act."[1] They gave the subject a thorough investigation, and summoned, among other witnesses, the town clerks of Leeds, Manchester, and Liverpool, leading returning officers, and election agents of both parties. The general and emphatic verdict was that a thorough change for the better had taken place. "All those disorders," said Sir Joseph Heron, town clerk of Manchester, "that used to occur under open voting have ceased altogether. . . . Any one walking through the borough would not know the fact that an election was going on; everything is so perfectly peaceful;" and yet "it was notorious that, taking the city as a whole, there was more interest felt in the elections than had been known for very many years

[1] Parl. Papers, 1876, vol. xii.

past." To the change in regard to the purity of the election he bears the strongest possible testimony: "I believe that such a thing as bribery does not exist at Manchester;" though it was in these large cities that the disorders of the previous decades had reached their extreme. "The ballot is a blessing to us," said the town clerk of Leeds, Mr. Curwood; and this testimony was corroborated on all sides.[1]

The course of legislation since 1872 indicates very

[1] Some fears had been expressed that the new method of marking the vote would have difficulties for the less intelligent voters, but the result showed this to be groundless. In a test vote taken by anticipation in Manchester in 1870, the total number of votes cast was 11,475, and of these only 80 were void for insufficient marking. At the Leeds election of 1874, out of 31,793 votes, only 86 were void for uncertainty or failure to mark; in the Kent election only 32 votes out of 23,000 were lost for uncertainty; and at Liverpool, in 1874, where 37,000 voted, the uncertain ballots were only 193 in number. These figures show a proportion of lost votes probably much lower (as polling-inspectors would testify) than the unknown number of miscarriages which occur in our present system in the awkward use of gummed pasters, or in attempting to erase individual names. All the English figures above quoted were those of the first election under the new system at the places named, and of localities where the illiterate vote reached its extreme, and in this light are even remarkable. There was also some testimony that at the election of 1876, with an increase of nearly 10 per cent in the number of voters, the number of votes rejected for the above reasons became smaller, showing that improper marking is not a constant attendant of the system, but as familiarity increases, tends to disappear. Australian experience also testified that very few votes were lost by mistake or informalities. In regard to the multiplicity of names upon a single ballot, it should be added that the conditions of English elections permit comparison with our own, for at School Board elections there are sometimes as many as 25 candidates. As respects polling arrangements under the new system, it was found that at the time of greatest pressure (and that under the cumbrous English provisions for taking the votes of illiterates) votes could be received at the rate of from 150 to 200 per hour, and this even where only four private compartments were provided at each polling-place.

clearly the degree to which the Ballot Act commended itself to the British people. In 1873 the Elementary Education Act (36 & 37 Vict., c. 86) provided for its application to the election of school boards;[1] and in 1884 the Education Department, by a General Order, combined its operation with the new method of cumulative voting. In 1875 the rules relating to municipal elections were revised by the Municipal Elections Act (38 and 39 Vict. c. 40) and in 1882 were placed, without material change, in the Municipal Corporations Act (45 & 46 Vict., c. 50). The Ballot Act was limited to expire Dec. 31, 1880, but it has been regularly continued in force from year to year,[2] and may now be regarded as a permanent element of the English electoral system. In August last it was applied to county elections by the Local Government Act, 1888 (51-52 Vict., c. 41), so that the entire field of elections in England and Wales, if not in Scotland and Ireland as well, is now covered by the Australian system of balloting.

Its success in this quarter had far-reaching results. The adoption of the system by Great Britain gave it a standing which it could not otherwise have had, and communities afflicted with like evils came to

---

[1] In 1870, the Education Act having given the Education Department power to hold elections in its own way, the ballot had been used at the School Board elections in London (Parl. Papers, 1884-85, vol. xi., Report of Com. on School Board Elections, (Voting)).

[2] 43-44 Vict , c. 48; 44-45 Vict., c. 70; 45-46 Vict., c. 61; 46-47 Vict., c. 40; 47-48 Vict., c. 53; 48-49 Vict., c. 59; 50 Vict., c. 5; 50-51 Vict., c. 63.

study the remedy which had there found favor. Naturally, the new method next appeared in Canada. It was adopted by the Legislative Assembly of the Province of Ontario, March 24, 1874 (Ballot Act, 37 Vict., c. 5); by the Dominion Parliament, May 26, 1874 (Dominion Elections Act, 37 Vict., c. 9), and by the Legislature of the Province of Quebec, February 23, 1875. Subsequent Dominion legislation has applied it to local option upon the temperance question (Canada Temperance Act, 1878, 41 Vict., c. 16). In Ontario it was immediately extended to municipal elections (38 Vict., c. 18, Dec. 21, 1874). In Quebec, where municipal elections have been governed by the Municipal Code of 1870, enacted while the old system was in force, the application of the Australian system to the city of Quebec by the charter recently granted (July 12, 1888, 51–52 Vict., c. 78), shows the growing demand, here as elsewhere, for the extension of the system to all manner of elections.[1]

---

[1] The following extracts from a letter by a Nova Scotian election officer, appearing in "The Nation" of Jan. 10, 1889, will be of interest: —

"In Canada the Australian ballot system has been in force for the past fourteen years. We have grown familiar with it, and what astonishes me is how any one can call it complex, or having once seen it could possibly endure to work with any other. . . . There are no provisions preventing persons congregating about the polling-booth. In practice it is found that the small polling district and the secret voting do away with all temptation to rioting. In former times here, with open voting and a few large sections, we had furious fights about the booths. . . . As to simplicity of working, there was a little difficulty at first, though nothing like what was predicted. But now very few mistakes are made or votes thrown away. . . . As to preventing bribery, it is not such a success as we should like. It has done a good

In Belgium also a remedy was needed for degenerate elections. The title of the Act of July 9, 1877, "*Sur le secret du vote et sur les fraudes électorales*," suggests the state of things which brought the subject to the attention of the legislature. Party spirit has always been high in Belgium. The great parties, Liberal and Catholic, were very evenly divided in this kingdom of six million souls, and the contest for the small number of votes which carried the balance of power gave birth to all forms of corruption, — to fraudulent registration, illegal voting, intimidation, improper influence, false counting, marked, altered, and suppressed ballots.[1] The modifications of the electoral law since the time of the constitution (1831) had been only recently codified in the Electoral Code of 1872; but England's example inspired a fresh movement of reform, and the Premièr, Malon, after a careful study of the Ballot Act of 1872, and suitable modification of its provisions, brought in, and succeeded in passing, the Act of July 9, 1877, — adopting substantially the English system in a much less cumbrous piece of legislation, but containing some unique improvements. This law applied only to national elections, but was in the succeeding year applied also to provincial and municipal elections;[2] and with the exception of one or two minor amend-

deal; nevertheless, the most of our bribable electors, especially in the country, make it a curious point of honor to vote the way they have been paid to. The Corrupt Practices Act . . . is far and away more effectual than the ballot."
"Halifax, N. S., Dec. 28."

[1] Annuaire de législation étrangère (Paris), vol. **xvii.**, 1877, p. 512.
[2] Annuaire, etc., vol. **xviii.**, 1878, p. 400.

ments (noticed in Part V., *infra*), has remained unaltered. In 1882 the various statutes were consolidated into a supplement to the Electoral Code of 1872.[1] In 1879 Belgium's diminutive neighbor, the Grand Duchy of Luxembourg (which, though nominally dependent on the Kingdom of the Netherlands, is practically autonomous, making and administering its own laws), in the law of May 28, bore witness to the efficient working of the Belgian measure by adopting it almost in its entirety;[2] and five years later, when the laws relating to elections were revised and codified, proved its own satisfaction with the system by applying it to municipal elections.[3]

Whether compulsory secrecy attended the ballot system introduced into Piedmont by Charles Albert in 1848, and into the kingdom of Italy in 1860 by Victor Emmanuel, the editor is not aware.[4] Cavour, who took an important part in the framing of the law, was always a champion and defender of at least permissive secrecy of voting; for it was, in his conviction, the only safeguard against clerical intimidation. But when the extension of the suffrage and electoral problems generally were discussed in 1881–82, and the question of the method of voting was reached, it would seem that the example of England and Belgium in pronouncing in favor of compulsory

---

[1] Supplément au code alphabétique des lois politiques, etc., par H. Wyvekens (Brussels, 1882).

[2] Annuaire. etc., vol. ix., 1879, p. 592.

[3] Act of Mar. 5, 1884: Annuaire, etc., vol. xiv., 1884, p. 527.

[4] See Parl. Papers, 1868–69, vol. viii., Test. of John W. Probyn, p. 583.

secrecy was in the minds of the framers of the law of 1882, and that its careful and detailed provisions for compulsory secrecy were influenced by the previous European legislation based on the Australian system. The electoral reforms of 1882 were comprised in the Acts of Jan. 22 and May 7, afterwards published as one by royal decree of Sept. 14.[1] They contain the essence of the Australian system. It will be noticed, however, that nominations are not required to be previously communicated to the authorities, since the official ballot is blank, and is written upon by the voter himself,[2] the candidates being made known beforehand at public meetings held in their interest, or by other methods of publication.

It remains to notice, in transatlantic governments, the adoption by Norway, in 1884,[3] of compulsory secrecy in voting. The time-honored custom in Norway, under the Electoral Act of 1828, had been to vote, at the pleasure of the elector, *viva voce* or by a signed ballot. In 1884 a system was adopted[4] nearly resembling the Italian method, but requiring the use of an official envelope; although, inasmuch as the voter procures his ballot for himself before entering the polling-place, the method is hardly to be considered as completely in accord with the Australian system.

The electoral statutes of certain other European

---

[1] Annuaire, etc., vol. xii., 1882, p. 503.
[2] A reading and writing qualification is imposed by the same Act of 1882.
[3] Act of July 1; Annuaire, etc., vol. xiv., 1884, p. 624.
[4] See part viii., L.

countries sometimes contain resemblances to the essential features of the Australian system. In Austria, for example, a blank official ballot-paper is used, and the vote is privately written; in France, Hungary, and Greece, pre-appointed nominations are required; but since in none of these states has the Australian system been adopted in its entirety, nor does the presence of this or that feature seem to have any historical connection with the Australian method, it would not be proper in this place to refer at length to those laws.[1]

In the Prussian Landtag the demand has been made, from time to time, for a secret ballot. Intimidation is common enough to need preventive measures of some sort; and, though the Government has as late as March, 1888, again failed to grant the reform,[2] it is probable that the movement must succeed before long.

The history of ballot reform in our own country is as yet brief, but is full of earnest and successful action on the part of its friends.

Of the movement in Louisville, Ky., which resulted in the Act of Feb. 24, 1888 (contained in Part VI., *infra*), the editor has no detailed information.[3] By this Act the Australian system, properly adapted, is applied to all elections of municipal officers in Louisville. In its working it has certainly accomplished

---

[1] See further, part viii., *infra*, N, and Charbonnier, Organisation électorale de tous les pays civilisés, Paris, 1883.

[2] Bulletin de la soc. de législ. comp., June, 1888, p. 611.

[3] See "The Nation," Dec. 13, 1888, containing a letter from a citizen of Louisville.

the results which were expected from it.[1] "The election last Tuesday," writes the correspondent in "The Nation," "was the first municipal election I

[1] The following letter testifying as to the operation of the law appeared in the Boston "Advertiser" and the Boston "Globe" of Jan. 11, 1889 : —

The law was apparently difficult and intricate. It had been predicted that the election would end in confusion and disorder. The chief local newspaper had given the project but cold support. Yet the event confounded all; it was administered with practically uniform ease and success by election officers who certainly did not rise above the average in intelligence. . . . I have heard of no case in which a ballot was thrown out in the count because of the failure of the voter to understand what was required of him.

In addition to demonstrating its perfect practicability, the election tested the power of the law to prevent bribery. It can hardly be possible that there is a city in the Union where open corruption has been more generally practised than in Louisville.

We do not admit the fact of its corruption without great regret; nor would we desire to be lulled into any false security respecting the efficacy of the means just tried to stamp it out. But it is an undeniable fact that in the late election there was, except in one place, no corruption successful, and but little attempted, and that with this evidence of its successful working the chances have greatly lessened that bribery will be tried.

Other objections that had been urged failed wholly to be justified. In no case, as far as I can learn, was there any delay in recording votes. A compartment is provided for every one hundred and seventy-five voters, whereas the Massachusetts law provides one for every seventy-five, and yet the accommodations were in every case ample. So far from interfering with the process of voting, I should not be surprised if actually less time were required than by the old *viva voce* system.

Again, the counting of votes proceeded apparently with perfect ease. The results of the election were published in the papers the following morning with the accustomed fulness; nor did the official count, so far as I know, require more time than was the case under the old method.

In some of its details the law may be improved, but in all essential particulars it is beneficent and effective, and we have seen enough to fix it firmly in the confidence of the people.

ABRAM FLEXUER.

Louisville, Ky., Jan. 3.

have ever known which was not bought outright. As a matter of fact no attempts at bribery were made."

In New York the movement had its rise simultaneously in several different sources. Mr. William M. Ivins, of New York, in "Electoral Reform, and the History of the Yates-Saxton Bill," says:—

"During the winter of 1887 the Commonwealth Club of New York, which consists of men of all shades of political faith, devoted a half-dozen meetings to the public consideration of the failure of the law to protect the suffrage, and at the end of the season appointed a committee of well-known and able lawyers and public men of large legislative and administrative experience to draft a bill for presentation to the legislature. Every one of these men was especially qualified for the work to do which he was appointed, and the committee as constituted consisted equally of Democrats and Republicans. This committee was subsequently joined by a like committee of the City Reform Club, appointed for the same purpose, and after many months of careful study prepared a measure which, after being approved by the Commonwealth Club, the Reform Club, the City Reform Club, and the Labor Party, was presented in the Assembly about the middle of the session of 1888, and known as the Yates Bill. Mr. Saxton and Mr. Hamilton had already presented bills looking to the same end. These bills were all referred to the Assembly Committee on Judiciary, and what was subsequently known as the Yates-Saxton, or Saxton, Bill was reported to the House. The bill, as reported, was substantially the Yates Bill with a few amendments adopted from the Hamilton and original Saxton bills, and this measure finally passed both Houses of the legislature."

It was vetoed, however, by Governor Hill. But although the veto checked for the moment legislation upon the subject, the movement has continued to increase in numbers and in strength. A Ballot Reform League has been formed, and a congress of the advocates of the reform in all the States is to be summoned during the year, for the purpose of achieving organization and concerted action, and for promoting uniformity and efficiency in the coming legislation. Meanwhile a new bill has been drafted and introduced[1] at the present legislative session, and upon this the friends of the reform expect to unite and to reach success.

The legislation of 1888 in Massachusetts was based on a popular movement even stronger and more widespread than that which made itself felt in New York. Bills were drawn by Messrs. Bailey, Dana, Hayes, and Whitmore, and were introduced early in the session of 1888. Petitions were received from the Common Council of Boston, from citizens of Boston, Cambridge, Chelsea, Fall River, Lynn, Newton, Somerville, Taunton, Worcester, and many of the rural districts, asking for similar legislation. The subject was laid before the joint committee on election laws, of which Henry H. Sprague, Esq., was chairman on the part of the Senate, and Alpheus Sanford, Esq., chairman on the part of the House; and it received exhaustive consideration. The Committee had before them the four bills above mentioned, the Saxton bill of New York, the Michigan bill (introduced in the legislative session of 1888 in Michigan, but lost through a failure of the two branches to agree), and the British, Canadian, and Australian statutes; and from this abundant material it was endeavored to shape a law which should be

[1] See Appendix I.

efficient and permanent, adapted to the electoral system of the State, and containing in its details the best features of previous legislation. The result of their work was a bill which, after slight alterations, was enacted by a practically unanimous vote, including the members of both leading parties, and was approved by the Governor May 30, 1888.[1]

[1] This was not the first time that the secret ballot had applied for admission to the Massachusetts statute book. The early ballot law of 1647, under which the vote was cast "by wrighting the names of the persons Elected, in papers open or once foulded, not twisted nor rowled up, that they may be the sooner perused" (Colonial Laws, 1672, "Elections," p. 47, reprint of 1887), was passed at a time when the distinction between a compulsory and an optional secrecy had not become important. By the year 1850 there was need enough for a measure of reform, and the Know-Nothing party took up the cause of the secret ballot, perhaps, to some extent, for the reason that secrecy in the political opinions of its members was almost necessary to the success of the movement. In 1850 a legislative committee, with Amasa Walker at its head, reported strongly in favor of a system of compulsory secrecy, which provided for furnishing official envelopes to all voters, and for counting no ballots not contained in the envelopes. This plan became a law in 1851 (c. 226), a coalition of Democrats and Free-soilers passing it by a small majority. The law seems to have worked well during its brief existence; although it is evident that practically it contains nothing to prevent bystanders from ascertaining what ballot is put into the envelope. But, in 1853, the Whigs again controlled the legislature, and on February 24 mortally wounded the new law by making it optional to demand or not an official envelope, as the voter pleased. To request an envelope thus ticketed the voter as clearly as could he wished. In May, 1853, a convention sat in Boston to propose amendments to the Constitution, and compulsory secrecy in voting was recommended as one of the amendments. The people, however, failed to accept it. In 1855 the American party carried the State, and, again passing the envelope bill in the House, were defeated in the Senate by one vote. At the time Charles Sumner was first elected to the U. S. Senate, an incident occurred on the joint ballot which created much comment at the time, and was used as an argument for the effectiveness of the secret ballot as a gauge of real conviction and a guarantee of liberty of action. After twenty-five fruitless ballotings, a motion was carried to place each ballot in a sealed

In Wisconsin, as a result of efforts towards reform, a law was passed in the session of 1887 regulating the conduct of elections in cities of more than 50,000 inhabitants, and incorporating some of the features of the Australian system. Preparation has been made in other States during the present winter for securing similar legislation. In Maine, a bill has been introduced at the present session of the legislature, by Mr. Looney of Portland, substantially the same in its provisions as the Massachusetts statute. The measure will be supported by prominent members of both leading parties, and by representatives of the Knights of Labor, and seems, here as elsewhere, to rest upon a strong popular demand. In Rhode Island a Ballot Reform Club has been organized, and a bill embodying the Australian system has been introduced at the present session of the legislature. In Michigan the efforts to secure legislation will doubtless be renewed. In addition to these States, the introduction of similar legislation is also in contemplation in California, Connecticut, New

---

envelope. Sumner was then elected on the twenty-sixth ballot. The optional envelope law is still in force in Massachusetts, but it is of no practical value, and is seldom taken advantage of.

The foregoing facts are drawn partly from two interesting pamphlets, — one, a letter from Amasa Walker to the Ballot Society of London, published by them in 1855 as Tract No. 5; the other, a modest essay by Edward L. Pierce of Milton, published in the Boston Post, of Aug. 2, 1852, republished in the Dedham Gazette, July 30, 1853, entitled " Secret Suffrage," afterwards reprinted by the Ballot Society, with notes by James Mill, and containing by far the best account (within the knowledge of the editor) of the secret ballot in classic times and of the history of the ballot reform movement in England down to 1855.

Jersey, Maryland, Virginia, Dakota, Delaware, Kansas, Tennessee, Indiana, Illinois, Ohio, New Hampshire, Pennsylvania, Montana, Nebraska, Colorado, Iowa, Louisiana, Missouri, Michigan, Wisconsin, and Oregon, and not improbably in others also. It would seem that, before many years pass, the entire electoral machinery of the country will have been reformed in accordance with the principles of the Australian method. That system has now received the approval of the legislatures of seventeen civilized states. Forty-five times these different legislatures have registered their approval of the system by various enactments (exclusive of amendments). The people who now conduct their elections by this machinery number nearly eighty-five millions; they are all citizens of free states, living under constitutional government, and enjoying representative institutions. So far, then, as its previous adoption has a significance, the system is shown to be neither an untested experiment, nor a questionable expedient drawn from dissimilar political experience; for it is not only well tried and long tried, but tested and adopted under political conditions and methods which we have in common with all representative governments. It is not the method of any one country or people, but finds a home wherever a pure and sincere expression of conviction is the constitutional mode of selecting the makers and the administrators of the laws.

II.

It remains briefly to suggest the reasons for the success of the Australian system, and a few of the special benefits which it promises to American politics. Amid the minor variations of detail in the numerous statutes, the cardinal features of the system, as everywhere adopted, are two: first, an arrangement for polling by which compulsory secrecy of voting is secured; second, an official ballot containing the names of all candidates, printed and distributed under state or municipal authority. Either of these may, on principle, exist without the other, although the second is almost indispensable as a part of the machinery for the perfect working of the first. Each requirement, however, has an efficiency of its own, and each operates against a special class of evils.

Let us glance at the first. The conditions of life among us now seem to be such that our statutory prohibitions, to be effective, must aim to operate chiefly by indirect methods. Statutes which seek to prevent by imposing a penalty are in numerous classes of cases practically of no effect, not only because satisfactory evidence of the violation is hard to obtain, but because, through public indifference or private favor, prosecutions for the offence are rare, — perhaps also because the prosecution of single offences cannot, in the nature of the offence, prove any serious check upon its repetition; perhaps also for other reasons. Whatever the causes, it has become apparent that the best results are to be reached, when preventive legislation is planned, by taking one of three courses: 1. By making the detection of the offence absolutely certain; 2. By taking away all interest in its commission, or by making it profitable to refrain; 3. By making the offence physically impossible. These methods, of late, are frequent in legislation, as an illustration or two will show. The screen law in force in many states is based on the first principle, and aims to make the sale of liquor so open that any violation of law can instantly be detected. The statutes requiring the registration of pawnbrokers' transactions and the rendering of accounts by public corporations, have a similar purpose. Again, acting upon the third principle, we find, for example, that the most effective way to prevent child labor in factories is to require the presence of the child at a school. If we look for an illustration of the second plan, we are reminded of the fire-escape and building-inspection laws, and the extreme difficulty which is found in enforcing their observance; yet when the insurance companies but suggest an increase of rates upon structures which violate the laws of safety, improvements are speedily made. In short, we have begun to realize that the mere printing of a penal statute is not the only step in prevention, and that the modern method must be the indirect method. The secret of effectively reaching an evil by law is either to insure its detection, to render it impossible, or to make it unprofitable.

Tedious as it may seem to dwell upon so obvious a matter, it has extreme importance for us, for this truth it is which underlies the effectiveness of the secret ballot and its usefulness for our political conditions. On the one hand it checks bribery and all those corrupt practices which consist in voting according to a bargain or understanding. No man has ever placed his money corruptly without satisfying himself that the vote was cast according to the agreement, or, in a phrase which became only too common during the last campaign, without proof that " the goods were delivered;" and when there is to be no proof but the word of the bribe-taker (who may have received thrice the sum to vote for the briber's opponent), it is idle to place any trust in such a use of money. In other words, take away all interest in committing an offence, and the offence will soon disappear. But this is trite and well-understood, and, in England and Australia, it is not merely a deduction made beforehand from our acquaintance with human nature, but an established fact of experience. On the other hand, the marking of the vote in seclusion reaches effectively another great class of evils, including violence and intimidation, improper influence, dictation by employers or organizations, the fear of ridicule and dislike, or of social or commercial injury, — all coercive influence of every sort depending on a knowledge of the voter's political action. Tumult and disorder at the polls, bargaining and trading of votes, and all questionable practices depending upon the knowledge gained, as the day goes on, of the drift of the contest, — it would hardly be necessary to argue in advance, even if England's experience did not prove it, that these practices, wherever they have prevailed, must disappear. In short, the secret ballot approaches these more or less elusive evils, not merely with the weak instrument of a penal clause for this and that offence, but with the effective methods of modern legislation. By compelling the dishonest man to mark his vote in secrecy, it renders it impossible for him to prove his dishonesty, and thus deprives him of the market for it. By compelling the honest man to vote in secrecy it relieves him not merely from the grosser forms of intimidation, but from more subtle and perhaps more pernicious coercion of every sort. By thus tending to eradicate corruption and by giving effect to each man's innermost belief, it secures to the Republic what at such a juncture is the thing vitally necessary to its health, — a free and honest expression of the convictions of every citizen.

I pass to the other essential feature of the Australian system, — a feature, if possible more important to the cause of good politics. This characteristic, it need hardly be said, is a development of the traditional method of nomination in England and Australia. But no long-meditated invention could have been more apt or more efficient to reach certain of the most pressing evils that attend our system of nominations. A rehearsal of them at this place is not needed, for they are familiar through experience to all citizens of our larger cities, and through hearsay, at least, to others.[1] "To find the honest men," says Mr. Bryce, in his recent work on "The American Commonwealth,"[2] "and having found them, to put them in office, and keep them there, is the great problem of American politics;" and one of the great reasons why they cannot be put there is, briefly, because the road is completely blocked; the extra-legal machinery which necessarily surrounds every election is in the complete possession, in the large cities, of a corrupt party machine, in too many other places, of party managers having more or less ignoble interests to serve; and the plain result is that since we have no opportunity to vote for the desirable men, we cannot of course elect them.

"Our elections," says Mr. Ivins, in his telling pamphlet on "Electoral Reform," "are not elections in any true sense of the word, and when we vote we simply register our choice as between two or three men who have already been elected by a machinery unknown to the law, a machinery which is really the personal property of the few, and in which the many have no right which they can enforce. The law being silent as to where the ballots are to come from, as to who shall supply and pay for them, and as to how they shall be distributed, a certain few in the community have created a Machine to do all these things, which the law necessitates, and does not provide for, and

---

[1] See "Machine Politics and Money in Elections in New York City," by Wm. B. Ivins; "Money in City Elections," by J. B. Bishop; A. C. Bernheim, in Pol. Sci. Quart. for March, 1888; F. W. Whitridge, article on "Assessments," in Amer. Cycl. Polit. Science; Dorman B. Eaton, article "Primary Elections," in the same work; Theodore Roosevelt, in "Century" for Nov., 1886; Henry George, in 136 N. Amer. Rev. (1883) 201; Bryce, "The American Commonwealth," ii. cc. 60-68, 88, 89.

[2] Vol. ii. p. 385.

have thereby actually put an end to the very political equality which the ballot is supposed to preserve inviolable. . . . Besides vesting the power of nomination in fee-simple in those persons who practically own the machinery for printing and distributing the ballots, the existing system amounts to an almost complete exclusion from official public life of all men who are not enabled to pay, if not a sum equal to the entire salary of the office they seek, at least a very large percentage of it. The poor man, the moderately well-to-do man, and the self-respecting and conscientious man are thus at once cut off from all political ambition, because the only key to success is wealth or machine power."

It is clear that the evil maintains itself because of the insufficiency of the election laws. Just so long as the law sanctions a method under which the only avenue to an election is through a nomination by a caucus or a convention, so long must we fail to elect the best men, for our hands are tied. "If a method can be found by which all men can be given political equality before the law, actually as well as theoretically, the evil will die a natural death." To compress the issue roughly into a phrase, — what we need now is not merely free elections, but free nominations also, — not merely a sincere and accurate expression of opinion, but an opportunity to nominate and to vote effectively for any one whom we desire.

This is why the method of nominations open to all and a place in the ballot free to all nominees is an integral and invaluable part of the Australian system of ballot reform. This is one reason why certain of the most glaring evils of popular government in this country have never fastened themselves upon the countries in which the method of open nominations prevails. This is why the ballot-reform movement promises to have effects far wider than the mere achievement of a single reform. It is the opening of a road (perhaps the only road) to the whole field of political improvements. For, if we solve by this means the great problem of our politics, if we are enabled to put honest and capable men in office and to keep them there, we shall have created legislative and administrative officers from whom we may expect the intelligent and fair consideration of those further improvements, — a sort of consideration which is now only exceptionally and (it may almost be said) accidentally accorded to them.[1]

---

[1] Mr. Ivins' summing up of the case is clear and succinct: "Let us therefore try to summarize distinctly the causes of the evil, and note the remedies which they naturally suggest: —

The Evil.

1. The necessity for voluntarily printing and distributing the ballot justifies organization for this purpose.
2. It practically vests the Machine with the monopoly of the election machinery;
3. And, as a consequence, with the monopoly of nomination.

The Remedy.

1. The printing and distribution of all ballots at public expense does away with the necessity of organization for this purpose.
2. And will deprive the political Machines of the monopoly of an essential part of the election machinery.
3. It will enable any body of citizens of the number prescribed by law to have the name of their candidate printed on the same ballot with the names of all other candidates for the same office, so that before the law and before the voters all candidates and all party organizations will stand on a perfectly even footing.

4. It involves the necessity of defraying the expenses of both printing and distribution by means of assessments on or contributions by candidates, office-holders, or party leaders,

5. Which facilitates bribery and corruption by affording them convenient covers;

6. And debauches the electors by leading them to become partisans for pay, instead of honestly and from conviction performing their duty as citizens.

4. This will dispense altogether with the necessity of and excuse for levying political assessments,

5. And leave no legal cover for bribery. The law can describe and limit all permissible expenditure, and compel the candidate or his agent to make a sworn return with vouchers to a proper public officer for all disbursements. It may punish all violations with sufficiently severe penalties,

6. And prescribe that no elector under pay of a party or candidate shall be permitted to vote, thus making it more the interest of candidates and parties not to pay than to pay for election services, and thus deterring all honest electors from accepting pay."

Wm. M. Ivins, in *" Electoral Reform."*

AUSTRALIAN BALLOT SYSTEM.

I. MASSACHUSETTS.

ACTS OF 1888.

CHAPTER 436.

AN ACT TO PROVIDE FOR PRINTING AND DISTRIBUTING BALLOTS AT THE PUBLIC EXPENSE, AND TO REGULATE VOTING AT STATE AND CITY ELECTIONS.

Be it enacted, etc., as follows:

SECTION 1. All ballots cast in elections for national, state, district, and county officers in cities and towns after the first day of November in the year eighteen hundred and eighty-nine, and all ballots cast in municipal elections in cities after that date, shall be printed and distributed at public expense, as hereinafter provided. The printing of the ballots and cards of instructions to voters shall in municipal elections in cities be paid for by the several cities respectively, and in all other elections the printing of the ballots and cards of instruction, and the delivery of them to the several cities and towns, shall be paid for by the Commonwealth. The distribution of the ballots to the voters shall be paid for by the cities and towns respectively. The term "state election," as used in this act, shall apply to any election held for the choice of a national, state, district, or county officer, whether for a full term or for the filling of a vacancy, and the term "state officer" shall apply to any person to be chosen by the qualified voters at such an election. The term "city election" shall apply to any municipal election so held in a city, and the term "city officer" shall apply to any person to be chosen by the qualified voters at such an election.

NOMINATIONS OF CANDIDATES.

SECT. 2. Any convention of delegates, and any caucus or meeting of qualified voters, as hereinafter defined, and individual voters to the number and in the manner hereinafter specified, may nominate candidates for public office, whose names shall be placed upon the ballots to be furnished as herein provided.

SECT. 3. Any convention of delegates representing a political party which, at the election next preceding, polled at least three per cent of the entire vote cast in the state, or in the electoral district or division thereof for which the nomination is made, or any convention of delegates who have been selected in caucuses called and held in accordance with a special statute providing therefor, and any caucus so called and held in any such electoral district or division, may for the state or for the district or division for which the convention or caucus is held, as the case may be, by causing a certificate of nomination to be duly filed, make one such nomination for each office therein to be filled at the election. Every such certificate of nomination shall state such facts as may be required as above for its acceptance, and as are required in section five of this act; shall be signed by the presiding officer and by the secretary of the convention or caucus, who shall add thereto their places of residence; and shall be sworn by them to be true to the best of their knowledge and belief, and a certificate of the oath shall be annexed to the certificate of nomination (*a*).

SECT. 4. Nominations of candidates for any offices to be filled by the voters of the state at large may be made by nomination papers signed in the aggregate for each candidate by not less than one thousand qualified voters (*a'*) of the state. Nominations of candidates for electoral dis-

(*a*) See NOTE 3, p. 54.

(*a'*) S. Austr., § 48; Queens., § 49;

tricts or divisions of the state may be made by nomination papers signed in the aggregate for each candidate by qualified voters of such district or division, not less in number than one for every one hundred persons who voted at the next preceding annual election in such district or division, but in no case less than fifty (*a*). In the case of a first election to be held in a town or ward newly established, the number of fifty shall be sufficient for the nomination of a candidate who is to be voted for only in such town or ward (*a*); and in the case of a first election in a district or division newly established, other than a town or ward, the number of fifty shall be so sufficient (*a*). Each voter signing a nomination paper shall add to his signature his place of residence, and each voter may subscribe to one nomination for each office to be filled, and no more. Women qualified to vote for members of the school committee may sign nomination papers for candidates for the school committee. The nomination papers shall before being filed be respectively submitted to the registrars of voters of the cities or towns in which the signers purport to be qualified voters, and each registrar to whom the same is submitted shall forthwith certify thereon what number of the signatures are names of qualified voters, both in the city or town for which he is a registrar, and in the district or division for which the nomination is made; one of the signers to each such separate paper shall swear that the statements therein are true, to the best of his knowledge and belief, and the certificate of such oath shall be annexed.

Gt. Br., A, § 1;
Belg., §§ 106, 155;
Ky., § 2;
N. Y., § 5;
and NOTE 2,
p. 53.

SECT. 5. All certificates of nomination and nomination papers shall, besides containing the names of candidates, specify as to each, (1) the office for which he is nominated; (2) the party or political principle which he represents, expressed in not more than three words; (3) his place of residence, with street and number thereon, if any. In the case of electors of president and vice-president of the United States, the names of the candidates for president and vice-president may be added to the party or political appellation.

SECT. 6. Certificates of nomination and nomination papers for the nomination of candidates for state offices shall be filed with the secretary (*b*) of the Commonwealth at least (*c*) fourteen days previous to the day of the election (*d*) for which the candidates are nominated. Such certificates and papers for the nomination of candidates for the offices of mayor and of aldermen in cities shall be filed with the city clerks (*b*) of the respective cities at least ten days (*d*) previous to the day of such election, and for the nomination of candidates for all other city offices at least six days (*d*) previous to the day of such election.

SECT. 7. The certificates of nomination and nomination papers being so filed, and being in apparent conformity with the provisions of this act, shall be deemed to be valid, unless objection thereto is duly made in writing. Such objections or other questions arising in relation thereto in the case of nominations of state officers shall be considered by (*e*) the secretary of the Commonwealth and the auditor and attorney-general, and the decision of the majority of these officers shall be final. Such objections or questions arising in the case of nominations of city officers shall be considered by (*e*) the board of registrars of voters, together with the city clerk, if not a member of such board, and the city solicitor; and the decision of a majority of these officers shall be final. In case such objection is made notice shall forthwith be mailed to the candidates affected thereby, addressed to their residences as given in the certificates of nomination or nomination papers (*e'*).

SECT. 8. Any person whose name has been presented as a candidate may cause his name to be withdrawn (*f*) from nomination, by request in writing signed by him and acknowledged before an officer qualified to take acknowledgments of deeds, and filed with the secretary of the Commonwealth ten days, or with the proper city clerk five days, as the case may be, previous to the day of election; and no name so withdrawn shall be printed upon the ballots. No nomination published and posted as herein provided shall be subsequently omitted as invalid.

MASSACHUSETTS. 41

SECT. 9. All certificates of nomination and nomination papers when filed shall be open under proper regulations to public inspection, and the secretary of the Commonwealth and the several city clerks shall preserve the same in their respective offices not less than five years.

FORM OF BALLOTS.

SECT. 10. Every general ballot, or ballot intended for the use of all male voters, which shall be printed in accordance with the provisions of this act, shall contain the names, residences, together with street and number, if any, and the party or political designation of all candidates whose nominations for any offices specified in the ballot have been duly made and not withdrawn in accordance herewith, and shall contain no other names. Except that in the case of electors of president and vice-president of the United States the names of the candidates for president and vice-president may be added to the party or political designation. / The names of candidates for each office shall be arranged (*g*) under the designation of the office in alphabetical order, according to surnames, except that the names of candidates for the offices of electors of president and vice-president shall be arranged in groups, as presented in the several certificates of nomination or nomination papers. There shall be left at the end of the list of candidates for each different office as many blank spaces as there are persons to be elected to such office, in which the voter may insert (*h*) the name of any person, not printed on the ballot, for whom he desires to vote as candidate for such office. Whenever the approval of a constitutional amendment or other question is submitted to the vote of the people, such questions shall be printed upon the ballot after the list of candidates. / Special ballots in cities, containing only the names of candidates for the school committee, shall also be prepared in like manner and printed for the use of women qualified according to law to vote for members of the school committee. The ballots shall be so printed as to give to each voter a clear

(*g*)
S. Austr., § 55;
Queens., § 58;
Gt. Br.,B, § 22,
D, § 1 (6);
Belg., §§ 114, 115;
Ky., § 4;
N.Y., § 14;
and NOTE 4,
p. 55.

(*h*)
Ky., § 9;
N.Y., § 13;
and NOTE 16,
p. 66.

opportunity to designate by a cross mark [×] in a sufficient margin at the right of the name of each candidate, his choice of candidates and his answer to the questions submitted, and on the ballot may be printed such words as will aid the voter to do this, as "vote for one," "vote for three," "yes,"· "no," and the like. The ballot shall be of the length now required by law (*i*) and two or more times such width. Before distribution the ballots shall be so folded in marked creases that their width and length when folded shall be those of the ballot now required by law. On the back and outside when folded, shall be printed "Official Ballot for," followed by the designation of the polling-place for which the ballot is prepared, the date of the election, and a fac-simile of the signature of the secretary of the Commonwealth or city clerk who has caused the ballot to be printed (*j*). The special ballots printed in cities for the use of women qualified to vote for school committee shall contain the additional endorsement that they are for such use only. Except as otherwise herein provided, ballots shall be printed in accordance with the existing provisions of law.

(*i*) Not more than 13¼ in., and not less than 12 in. (1884, c. 299, § 27).

(*j*) S. Austr., § 57; Queens., § 71; Gt. Br., A, § 2, B. § 24; Belg., §§ 123, 151; Ky., §§ 4, 7; N. Y. § 21, and NOTE 7, p. 59.

SECT. 11. All ballots when printed shall be folded as hereinbefore provided and fastened together in convenient numbers in books or blocks, in such manner that each ballot may be detached and removed separately. A record of the number of ballots printed and furnished to each polling-place shall be kept and preserved by the secretary of the Commonwealth and the several city clerks.

SECT. 12. There shall be provided for each voting place, at which an election is to be held, two sets of such general ballots, each of not less than one hundred for every fifty and fraction of fifty registered male voters therein (*k*), and likewise two sets of such special ballots, each of not less than one hundred, for every fifty and fraction of fifty women qualified to vote for school committee therein; and it shall be the duty of the registrars of voters in each city or town in which an election for state officers is to be held, to certify to the secretary of the

(*k*) S. Austr., § 56; Queens., § 58; Ky., § 3; N. Y., § 16.

Commonwealth fourteen days previous to any such election, the number of male registered voters in each voting precinct or in each town which is not divided into voting precincts, and in cities the number of women so registered as voters.

INFORMATION TO VOTERS.

SECT. 13. The secretary of the Commonwealth, in case of a State election, and the several city clerks, in case of city elections, shall prepare full instructions for the guidance of voters at such elections, as to obtaining ballots, as to the manner of marking them, and the method of gaining assistance, and as to obtaining new ballots in place of those accidentally spoiled, and they shall respectively cause the same, together with copies of sections twenty-seven, twenty-eight, twenty-nine, and thirty of this Act to be printed in large, clear type, on separate cards, to be called cards of instructions; and they shall respectively furnish the same and the ballots for use in each such election. They shall also cause to be printed on tinted paper, and without the fac-simile indorsements, ten or more copies of the form of the ballot provided for each voting place at each election therein, which shall be called specimen ballots, and shall be furnished with the other ballots provided for each such voting place.

SECT. 14. The secretary of the Commonwealth shall, six days at least previous to the day of any election of State officers, transmit to the registrars of voters in each city and town in which such election is to be held, printed lists containing the names, residences, and party or political appellations of all candidates nominated as herein provided for such election, and to be voted for at each polling place in each such city and town respectively, substantially in the form of the general ballot to be so used therein; and the registrars of voters shall immediately cause the lists for each town or voting precinct, as the case may be, to be conspicuously posted (*l*) in one or more public places in such town or voting precinct. The secretary of the Commonwealth shall likewise cause to be published (*l*) prior to the day of any such election, in at least two newspapers, if there be so many, published in each county, representing, as far as practicable, the political parties which, at the preceding election, cast the largest and next largest number of votes, a list of all the nominations made as herein provided, and to be voted for in such county, so far as may be, in the form in which they shall appear upon the general ballots.

(*l*)
S. Austr., § 50;
Queens., §§ 50, 53;
Gt. Br., B, § 9,
D, § 1 (3);
Belg., § 112;
Ky., § 5;
N. Y., § 10.

SECT. 15. The city clerk of each city shall four days at least prior to the day of any city election therein, cause to be conspicuously posted (*l*) in one or more public places in each voting precinct of such city a printed list containing the names, residences, and party or political appellations of all candidates nominated, as herein provided, and to be voted for in such precinct, substantially in the form of the general ballot to be so used therein; and he shall likewise cause to be published (*l*), prior to the day of such election in at least two newspapers, if there be so many, published in such city, representing the political parties which cast at the preceding election the largest and next largest number of votes, a list of all the nominations made, as herein provided, and to be voted for in such city, so far as may be, in the form in which they shall appear upon the general ballots.

DELIVERY OF BALLOTS TO CITIES AND TOWNS.

SECT. 16. The secretary of the Commonwealth shall send, separately and at different times or by different methods, the two sets of general and special ballots, together with the specimen ballots and cards of instruction printed by him, as herein provided, to the several city and town clerks, so as to be received by them, one set forty-eight hours at least previous to the day of election, and the other set twenty-four hours at least previous thereto. The same shall be sent in sealed packages, with marks on the outside clearly designating the polling-place for which they are intended and the number of ballots of each kind enclosed; and the respective city and town clerks shall on delivery to them of such packages return receipts therefor to the secretary. The secretary shall keep a record of the time when, and the manner in which the several packages are sent, and shall preserve for the period of one year the receipts of the city and town clerks.

SECT. 17. The two sets of ballots, together with the specimen ballots and cards of instruction printed by the city clerks, as herein provided, shall be packed by them in separate sealed packages, with marks on the outside clearly designating the polling precincts for which they are intended, and the number of ballots of each kind enclosed.

SECT. 18. The several city and town clerks shall send to the election officers of each voting-place before the opening of the polls on the day of election one set of ballots so prepared, sealed, and marked for such voting-place, and a receipt of such delivery shall be returned to them from the presiding or senior election officer present, which receipt, with a record of the number of ballots sent, shall be kept in the clerks' office. At the opening of the polls in each polling-place the seals of the packages shall be publicly broken, and the packages shall be opened by the presiding election officer, and the books or blocks of ballots shall be delivered to the ballot officers hereinafter provided for. The cards of instruction shall be immediately posted at or in each voting shelf or compartment provided in accordance with this act for the marking of the ballots, and not less than three such cards and not less than five specimen ballots shall be immediately posted in or about the polling-room, outside the guard-rails. The second set of ballots shall be retained by the respective clerks until they are called for or needed for the purposes of voting, and, upon the requisition in writing of the presiding election officer of any voting-place, the second set of ballots shall be furnished to such voting-place in the manner above provided as to the first set.

SECT. 19. In case the ballots to be furnished to any city

or town or voting-place therein, in accordance with the provisions of this act, shall fail for any reason to be duly delivered, or in case after delivery they shall be destroyed or stolen, it shall be the duty of the clerk of such city or town to cause other ballots to be prepared substantially in the form of the ballots so wanting and to be furnished; and upon receipt of such other ballots from him, accompanied by a statement under oath that the same have been so prepared and furnished by him, and that the original ballots have so failed to be received or have been so destroyed or stolen, the election officers shall cause the ballots so substituted to be used in lieu of the ballots wanting, as above.

ADDITIONAL ELECTION OFFICERS.

SECT. 20. Two inspectors, with two deputy inspectors, additional to those now provided for (*m*), shall be appointed in each voting precinct in cities and in towns divided into voting precincts, and the provisions of law relative to inspectors and deputy inspectors shall be applicable to such additional officers. Two of the inspectors acting in each voting precinct shall be detailed to act as ballot clerks. In towns not divided into voting precincts, two inspectors, with deputy inspectors, shall be appointed, in accordance with the provisions of law applicable to such officers in towns so divided, and the two inspectors thus serving shall act as ballot clerks. The two ballot clerks detailed and appointed as above in each voting precinct and town shall have the charge of the ballots therein, and shall furnish them to the voters in the manner hereinafter set forth. A duplicate list of the qualified voters in each precinct and each town not divided into precincts shall be prepared for the use of the ballot clerks, and all the provisions of law relative to the preparation, furnishing, and preservation of check-lists shall apply to such duplicate lists.

(*m*) Viz., a warden, clerk, and two inspectors. The deputy officers act as substitutes only.

VOTING SHELVES OR COMPARTMENTS.

SECT. 21. The officers in each city or town whose duty it is to designate and appoint polling-places therein shall

MASSACHUSETTS. 47

cause the same to be suitably provided with a sufficient number of voting shelves or compartments (*n*), at or in which voters may conveniently mark their ballots, so that in the marking thereof they may be screened from the observation of others, and a guard-rail shall be so constructed and placed that only such persons as are inside said rail can approach within six feet of the ballot-boxes and of such voting shelves or compartments. The arrangement shall be such that neither the ballot-boxes nor the voting shelves or compartments shall be hidden from view of those just outside the said guard-rail. The number of such voting shelves or compartments shall not be less than one for every seventy-five voters qualified to vote at such polling-place, and not less than three in any town or precinct thereof, and not less than ten in any voting precinct of a city (*o*). No persons other than the election officers and voters admitted as hereinafter provided shall be permitted within said rail (*p*), except by authority of the election officers for the purpose of keeping order and enforcing the law. Each voting shelf or compartment shall be kept provided with proper supplies and conveniences for marking the ballots.

(*n*) S. Austr., § 54; Queens., § 59; Gt. Br., B. § 16; Belg., § 117; Ky., § 8; N. Y., § 20; and NOTE 5, p. 58.

(*o*) Queens., § 59; Gt. Br., B. § 16; Belg., § 118; Ky., § 8; N. Y., § 20.

(*p*) S. Austr., § 59; Queens., § 59; Gt. Br., B. § 21; Belg., § 97; Ky., § 17; N. Y., § 20; and NOTE 1, p. 52.

PREPARATION OF BALLOTS.

SECT. 22. Any person desiring to vote shall give his name, and, if requested so to do, his residence, to one of the ballot clerks, who shall thereupon announce the same in a loud and distinct tone of voice, clear and audible, and if such name is found upon the check-list by the ballot officer having charge thereof, he shall likewise repeat the said name, and the voter shall be allowed to enter the space enclosed by the guard-rail as above provided. The ballot clerk (*q*) shall give him one, and only one, ballot, and his name shall be immediately checked on said list. If the voter is a woman, she shall receive a special ballot containing the names of candidates for school committee only. Besides the election officers, not more than four voters in excess of the number of voting shelves or compartments

(*q*) S. Austr., § 58, IV.; Queens., § 71; Gt. Br., B. § 50; Belg., § 123; Ky., § 7; N. Y., § 21; and NOTE 6, p. 59.

provided shall be allowed in said enclosed space at time.

SECT. 23. On receipt of his ballot the voter shall forthwith, and without leaving the enclosed space, retire alone to one of the voting shelves or compartments so provided and shall prepare his ballot by marking (*r*) in the appropriate margin or place, a cross [×] opposite the name of the candidate of his choice for each office to be filled, or by filling in the name of the candidate of his choice in the blank space provided therefor, and marking a cross [×] opposite thereto; (*r*) and, in case of a question submitted to the vote of the people, by marking in the appropriate margin or place, a cross [×] against the answer which he desires to give. Before leaving the voting shelf or compartment the voter shall fold his ballot, without displaying the marks thereon, in the same way it was folded when received by him, and he shall keep the same so folded until he has voted. He shall vote in the manner now provided by law (*s*) before leaving the enclosed space, and shall deposit his ballot in the box with the official endorsement uppermost. He shall mark and deposit his ballot without undue delay and shall quit said enclosed space as soon as he has voted. No such voter shall be allowed to occupy a voting shelf or compartment already occupied by another, nor to remain within said enclosed space more than ten minutes (*t*), nor to occupy a voting shelf or compartment for more than five minutes in case all of such shelves or compartments are in use, and other voters are waiting to occupy the same. No voter not an election officer whose name has been checked on the list of the ballot officers, shall be allowed to re-enter said enclosed space during said election. It shall be the duty of the presiding election officer for the time being to secure the observance of the provisions of this section.

SECT. 24. No person shall take or remove any ballot from the polling-place before the close of the polls. If any voter spoils a ballot (*u*) he may successively obtain others one at a time, not exceeding three in all, upon re-

---

(*r*)
S. Austr., § 58,
VI.;
Queens., § 73;
Gt. Br., A, § 2,
B, § 25; C.
"Form of Directions for Voters;"
Belg., A, § 124;
B, § 1;
Ky., § 9;
N. Y., § 22;
and NOTE 9,
p. 62.

(*s*)
The voter gives his name to the presiding officer, who announces it in a loud voice; the officer in charge of the list finds and repeats it; and the voter then deposits his ballot (1884, c. 299, § 17).

(*t*)
Ky., § 12;
N. Y., § 23.

(*u*)
S. Austr., § 58,
VIII.;

MASSACHUSETTS.   49

and each spoiled one. The ballots thus returned shall be immediately cancelled, and together with those not distributed to the voters, shall be preserved and with the check-list used by the ballot clerks, which shall be certified by them to be such, shall be secured in an envelope, sealed, and sent to the several city and town clerks, as required by law in the case of the ballots cast, and the other check-list used.

Gt. Br., B, § 28;
Belg., § 125;
Ky., § 9;
N. Y., § 24.

SECT. 25. Any voter who declares to the presiding election officer that he was a voter prior to the first day of May in the year eighteen hundred and fifty-seven, and cannot read (*v*), or that by blindness or other physical disability he is unable to mark his ballot (*v*), shall, upon request, receive the assistance of one or two of the election officers in the marking thereof, and such officer or officers shall certify on the outside thereof that it was so marked with his or their assistance, and shall thereafter give no information regarding the same. The presiding officer may in his discretion require such declaration of disability to be made by the voter under oath before him, and he is hereby qualified to administer the same.

(*r*)
S. Austr., § 58, VII;
Queens., § 73;
Gt. Br., B, § 26;
Belg., § 123;
Ky., § 10;
N. Y., § 25;
and NOTE 8, p. 61.

SECT. 26. If the voter marks more names than there are persons to be elected to an office, or if for any reason it is impossible to determine the voter's choice for any office to be filled, his ballot shall not be counted for such office. No ballot without the official endorsement shall, except as herein otherwise provided, be allowed to be deposited in the ballot-box, and none but ballots provided in accordance with the provisions of this act shall be counted (*w*). Ballots not counted shall be marked "defective" on the back thereof, and shall be preserved.

(*w*)
S. Austr., § 64;
Queens., § 76;
Gt. Br., A, § 2;
Belg., §§ 124, 147;
Ky., § 11;
N. Y., §§ 13, 28; and NOTE 10, p. 63.

PENALTIES.

SECT. 27. A voter who shall, except as herein otherwise provided, allow his ballot to be seen by any person with an apparent intention of letting it be known how he is about to vote, or who shall make a false statement as to his inability to mark his ballot, or any person who shall interfere, or attempt to interfere with any voter when inside said enclosed space or when marking ballot, or who shall endeavor to induce any voter before voting to show how he marks or has marked his ballot, shall be punished by fine of not less than five dollars nor more than one hundred dollars ; and election officers shall report any person so doing to the police officer in charge of the polls, whose duty it shall be to see that the offender is duly brought before the proper court.

SECT. 28. Any person who shall, prior to an election, wilfully deface or destroy any list of candidates posted in accordance with the provisions of this act, or who, during an election, shall wilfully deface, tear down, remove or destroy any card of instruction or specimen ballot printed or posted for the instruction of voters, or who shall during an election wilfully remove or destroy any of the supplies or conveniences furnished to enable a voter to prepare his ballot, or shall wilfully hinder the voting of others, shall be punished by fine of not less than five dollars nor more than one hundred dollars.

SECT. 29. Any person who shall falsely make or wilfully deface or destroy any certificate of nomination or nomination-paper, or any part thereof, or any letter of withdrawal ; or file any certificate of nomination or nomination-paper or letter of withdrawal, knowing the same or any part thereof to be falsely made ; or suppress any certificate of nomination or nomination-paper, or any part thereof which has been duly filed ; or forge or falsely make the official endorsement on any ballot ; or wilfully destroy or deface any ballot, or wilfully delay the delivery of any ballots, shall be punished by fine not exceeding one thousand dollars, or by imprisonment in the jail not more than one year, or by both such fine and imprisonment.

SECT. 30. Any public officer upon whom a duty is imposed by this act, who shall wilfully neglect to perform such duty (x), or who shall wilfully perform it in such a way as to hinder the objects of this act (x), shall be punished by fine of not less than five nor more than one

(x)
S. Austr., § 85;
Queens., § 120;

MASSACHUSETTS. 51

thousand dollars, or by imprisonment in jail for not more than one year, or by both such fine and imprisonment. *Approved May* 29, 1888.

_{Gt. Br., A, § 11; N. Y., § 31; and NOTE 11, p. 64.}

(*a.*)

FORM OF BALLOT USED UNDER THE ABOVE ACT.

(See the model at the end of the book.)

(*b.*)

POLLING ARRANGEMENTS UNDER THE ABOVE ACT.

The voter enters at the right-hand lower corner, receives his ballot from a ballot officer (not shown in this sketch), and then goes to the shelves, where he finds full instructions posted. He there marks and folds his ballot, and on his way out deposits it in the ballot-box in front of the election officers, as shown.

Note 1.

Presence of the Public at the Polls.

(Mass., § 21; S. Austr., § 50; Queens., § 50; Gt. Brit., B, § 21; Belg , § 97; Ky., §§ 17, 18; N. Y., §§ 20, 32.)

The provisions intended to prevent disorder and undue solicitation at the polls vary in strictness: — 1. In Massachusetts the public are excluded only from the railed space within the voting-room; that is, only from a space reasonably sufficient to ensure secrecy in marking the vote. 2. In South Australia, Queensland, Kentucky, Great Britain, and Belgium, the public are excluded from the entire polling-room. 3. In New York, the public are excluded from the railed space, and, in addition, "electioneering," presumably including solicitation, canvassing, etc., is forbidden within one hundred feet of the polling-room. The strong objection to the exclusion of the public from the entire room is that it leaves the purity of the election entirely in the hands of the agents or inspectors of the respective parties; for in order to perpetrate almost every fraud it would only be necessary to buy up the election officers of the opposite party. Still more undesirable is such a regulation in the interest of independent candidates, who in most States are not allowed to be represented by separate inspectors; the independent vote, by an arrangement between the agents of the two leading parties, could easily be disposed of (as the recent example of a far Western city indicates). Reasons of safety make it absolutely indispensable that access to a reasonable portion of the voting-room should be permitted to any and every citizen during the entire course of the election. If it is objected that the directions by an illiterate to the officer for marking his vote are, as in the English Act, required to be made aloud in the presence of the representatives of each party, and would be heard by every one present, if the public were admitted, the answer is that these can be and should be made privately in one of the compartments to (as in Massachusetts) a single representative, selected by the voter himself.

The best plan would seem to be, as in New York, to (1) exclude the public from the railed space only; (2) forbid solicitation or canvassing of any sort in the remainder of the polling-room, and within one hundred feet from the exterior.

Note 2.

Number of Electors necessary for a Nomination.

(Mass., § 4; S. Austr., § 48; Queens., §§ 48, 49; Gt. Brit., A, § 1;
Belg., §§ 106, 155; Ky., § 2; N. Y., § 5.)

In determining the number of signatures necessary to be obtained in order to put a candidate in nomination, the single object is of course to place all on a practically equal footing, and to impose only such restrictions as are necessary to prevent the ballot from being encumbered with the names of unbalanced persons and men of straw. But even though (as in Massachusetts) a minimum of fifty be established, very few aspirants will be found who cannot muster a sufficient number of names; and the better way, since the number of signatures is practically no hindrance, is to place the required number as low even as in South Australia (two), and thus, while losing no benefit, avoid even that appearance of exclusiveness for which the Massachusetts law has sometimes been attacked. The real restrictions on the number of candidates will be found to be, as English and Australian experience shows, public opinion and the interests of the aspirants. The former will throw ridicule on a candidacy which has no support; and the latter will, as now, have a powerful deterrent influence wherever there is not some strong ground for the candidacy.

A reason in England for fixing the number of signatures as low as ten seems to have been the desire not to pledge or to make public the political action of a larger number of electors. This would be a serious consideration where, as formerly in Greece,[1] a nomination-paper must contain the signatures of one-twentieth of the electors of the district; and even under the Massachusetts law, if three nominations for a city council are made in a ward containing 1200 electors or less, an opportunity is offered for coercing 150 electors into a virtual pledge which they may consider morally binding upon them at the polls. It would seem to be better to require as few names as possible, — perhaps not more than ten, — thus losing nothing, and avoiding certain probable disadvantages.

[1] Parl. Papers, 1868-9, vol. viii., p. 416; for the present rule, see Part VIII., N., *infra*.

In Queensland (§ 55) the device of requiring a deposit, to be returned to candidates receiving one-fifth the vote of the successful candidate having the smallest number of votes, has been adopted for the purpose of limiting the number of candidates. This may be expedient enough under the political conditions of some communities; but it is to be remembered that in this country a candidacy may be hopeless as regards the election of the nominee, and yet important and highly desirable as a means of exhibiting the strength of a section of electors or of a particular movement, and of thus compelling the attention of the leading parties and the modification of their platforms and legislative policies.[1] The Queensland provision would bear unfairly, for example, upon the labor vote and the prohibition vote in many States,— to name no other movements whose only hope frequently lies in emphasizing their growing strength by the figures of their vote and demanding a due consideration. It would seem, therefore, that the plan of requiring a returnable deposit is not adapted to our political methods, and that its adoption would be ill-advised.

Note 3.

Acceptance of the Nomination.

(S. Austr., § 48; Belg., § 107)

An acceptance of the nomination is required by two only of the seven principal statutes; but it ought to be a general requirement. In the first place, wherever a security for the expenses of election is required, an acceptance is desirable in order to avoid disputes as to the responsibility of the candidate or his nominators. Secondly, it prevents the unauthorized use of a prominent name, and the difficulties that might ensue in such a case. Thirdly, it places on record the deliberate decision of the nominee to appear as a candidate, and thus, while not preventing a withdrawal for good reasons, it places the burden of explanation upon one who withdraws, and throws difficulties in the way of a withdrawal for improper reasons, and of such " deals " and other political tricks as are now only too common. In the same way, it tends to prevent the practice of

---

[1] See Bryce, Amer. Commonwealth, ii. 222, where the importance of minority protests is touched upon.

putting up a candidate for the sole purpose of withdrawing him for a consideration to be received from opposing interests. Any regulation which tends to make public the reasons for withdrawal is a good one, for proper reasons will not fear publicity.

NOTE 4.

Arrangement of Contents of Ballot.

(Mass., § 10; S. Austr., § 55; Queens., § 58; Gt. Brit., B, § 22; D, § 1 (6); Belg., §§ 114, 115; Ky., § 4; N. Y., § 14.)

The arrangement of the contents of the ballot offers a large field for difference of opinion, although it may be suggested that any intelligent arrangement will answer the purpose, and that the importance of the different variations that have been adopted is practically not very great. Some of the more noticeable differences of method will be commented on.

1. In the beginning the question presents itself whether the names shall be arranged, as in Belgium and New York, in groups representing the nominations of one party for all offices, or as in Canada (see Part VIII., G.), Kentucky, and Massachusetts, in groups representing all nominations for the same office, the order of names being alphabetical. The principal consideration in favor of the former mode is that where a reading and writing qualification does not exist, it greatly helps the illiterate voter; for this plan allows a vote to be given for all the candidates of one party by making a single cross at the head of the list, and as the illiterate will know beforehand the position of his party list, he has only to make his cross there and the matter is ended. This consideration would entirely disappear in view of the clause (which presumably would be found in most statutes) permitting assistance to be given to illiterates by election officers, were it not for a fact brought out by English experience. It is that many illiterates, disliking to make confession and ask assistance, prefer to take the ballot and guess at the name they wish to mark. If this class of voters could be shown to include any appreciable number, their protection ought to be considered; although it may be questioned whether a plan otherwise desirable should be rejected for the sake of those who, by refusing to acknowledge the fact of their illiteracy, voluntarily expose themselves to mistake. Another consideration in favor

of the first method is that the marking of the vote for those who desire to vote an entire ticket is simpler and speedier. It is to be observed, however, not only that this gain would not affect those electors who vote independently of party, but that for the voter who goes outside of the party ticket for so much as a single name (and these voters may be roughly estimated at one third or more of the whole number) this mode of arrangement has no advantages, since he must in that case mark individually each of the remaining party candidates for whom he votes, though they fall short one only of the entire number.

A serious objection to the first method is that it may in many cases be impracticable. Any one who will refer to the discussions in the Belgian Chamber[1] will see what disputes they fell into, within a year after putting the system into operation, over the expediency of this method. It applies well enough where two parties only are in the field. But when independent candidates are named, and other parties make nominations, its difficulty is that it becomes cumbrous, and, unless the New York system of printing separate ballots, six or seven in all, for different classes of offices, is adopted, it may prove absolutely impracticable. Even the adoption of the separate ballot system of New York might to some seem only the substitution of one piece of unwieldy machinery for another. A second objection is that where, as in many places at elections of local officers, the national party lines are not drawn, this method becomes useless and out of place. A list of candidates for all such offices is usually nominated by a single convention or committee, but it does not always have coherency, and the personal merits of each candidate generally determine the electors' action.

Other objections also suggest themselves. The first plan tends to foster a sheep-like and unintelligent manner of voting for the local offices. The voter quickly marks the entire list of his party, and if on the same ballot are the names of candidates for the lesser and local offices, whose needs are governed by perhaps an entirely different set of considerations, no suggestion of this is brought to the voter's mind, but he is incited to judge the needs of the nation and of the county by one and the same test of policy and in one and the same mental effort. It may also be suggested that in one or two ways it operates unfairly upon

---

[1] Annuaire de légis. étrang., vol. xviii., 1878, notes to pp. 406, *et seq.*

individual candidates. It forces them to declare absolutely for one party or another, while they may in fact prefer to sail under a compromise name, such as "Labor Democrat," and yet would rather stand in a party list than be numbered among the independents. It also handicaps a popular candidate for a lesser office by (to a great extent) influencing the sheep-like voters of the opposite party to overlook their own candidate for the lesser office, and by thus confining the popular candidate to his strict party vote, which may fall far short of a plurality. Moreover, the list of independent candidates, as it appears by the side of the full party lists, suffers in moral weight (for want of a better phrase), has a detached and uninviting appearance, depriving them of that equal footing which it is the great design of the system that every candidate should have. These objections, it may be answered, apply equally to the present system of voting by tickets. They do; and it is simply because the people wish to do away with the inequalities and injustice of that system that we should hesitate to use a method of party lists which retains some of the same imperfections. It is a method vastly in advance of the present system; but it is not perfect, while the plan employed in Massachusetts, Kentucky, and Canada, though not perfect, is certainly free from the objections that have been mentioned. *Perfect equality upon the ballot-paper for all candidates* is what should be insisted upon.[1]

2. In making provision for the benefit of illiterates, other expedients have also been adopted. In England, Belgium, and Quebec (see Part VIII., II), a number is placed to the left of each candidate's name. In Ontario, for elections to the Provincial Assembly, each candidate's name is printed in a different color (Part VIII., G). In Belgium (Part V.) the Liberal names are printed in blue ink, the Catholic names in carmine, and the independent nominees in black. The plan of using figures would seem a satisfactory one, although it would be practically useless where, as at most elections, a large number of offices are to be filled, and the voter could not memorize the

---

[1] The editor will state, as his impression, that the party list method, as adopted by the New York legislature, was a compromise measure (one, at least, of the three bills there introduced being not much more than a sop thrown to reform), and that this method, as finally incorporated in the bill would not be considered as the best by the friends of the system, but only as the best that could be secured.

order of the names for each office. The color device is also an effective one; but it would be expensive, and is apt to foster a rivalry based on party emblems rather than on party principles. All these contrivances seem to be unnecessary wherever the election officers are required to give assistance to illiterates, and would cumber the ballot to no good purpose.

3. The Massachusetts ballot, an example of which is appended to this volume, shows the feasibility of placing the names of all candidates upon one ballot. If city offices are also to be filled at the same election (a practice which ought to be discontinued, as it has been in Massachusetts), or if presidential electors ("useless cogwheels" that will before long be swept away) are to be elected, the names may be placed on a separate ballot, or may be placed on an additional fold of the same ballot (as the Massachusetts law provides). Whether the titles of the offices should be placed, as in Kentucky (Part VI.) and Ontario (Part VIII., G), at the side of the group of candidates, or horizontally above each group, as in Massachusetts, is not a matter of much moment; but the latter would seem to be the method most convenient, and most in accord with the present customary arrangement, which should be followed so far as possible.

NOTE 5.

Arrangement of the Polling-Room.

(Mass., § 21; S. Austr., § 54; Queens., § 59; Gt. Brit., B, § 16; Belg., § 117; Ky., § 8; N. Y., § 20.)

A very simple and inexpensive structure will suffice to furnish entire secrecy in marking the ballot. Perhaps the arrangement shown in the illustration (*supra*, p. 51) is as good as any. In Kentucky the compartment resembles a sentry-box, and the voter enters and closes the door. It would seem that by this plan very little light would be furnished for marking the ballot. There is, however, a more serious objection. While the act of marking should be screened from all observation, yet the person of the voter should remain in plain sight. This is necessary in order to prevent attempts at fraud, — substitution of non-official ballot, exhibiting the ballot, etc.; and is provided for by the Massachusetts plan of arrangement. The voter's person should be in sight, not only while marking his ballot, but during the entire

NOTES.   59

period from the time of receiving the ballot to the time of depositing it; and therefore the plan sometimes adopted in England (and provided for by the Wisconsin law, Part VIII., 1.) of using one room for receiving and depositing the ballot, and an adjoining room for marking the vote, is not desirable. The simplest and safest arrangement seems to be that shown in the illustration above, by which the voter, entering at one gate, passes around and deposits his vote, without once retracing his steps or leaving the room.

NOTE 6.

Delivery of the Ballot.

(Mass., § 22; S. Austr., § 58, IV.; Queens., § 71; Gt. Brit., B, § 50; Belg., § 123; Ky., § 7; N. Y., § 21.)

If the Massachusetts polling arrangement be adopted, the ballot clerk will of course be the officer to deliver the ballots to voters, while the presiding officer attends to the business of receiving ballots. But this division of labor should in any case be insisted upon. Three of the above statutes place both duties upon the presiding officer; but it is manifestly impossible that while attending to his principal duty of questioning voters, receiving the ballots, and verifying the official mark upon them, he can at the same time properly distribute ballots to those applying for them.

NOTE 7.

Identification of Official Ballot.

(Mass., § 10; S. Austr., § 57; Queens., § 71; Gt. Brit., A, § 2, B, § 24; Belg., §§ 123, 151; Ky., §§ 4, 7; N. Y., § 21.)

An examination of the above sections will show the variety of the modes adopted by the different legislatures for guarding against frauds in connection with the ballot. Each method will sufficiently suggest its special advantages or drawbacks; but a few points of difference may here be noted: —

1. Whether the official mark should be placed on all the ballots before the opening of the polls (as in Massachusetts) or upon each one immediately before delivery to the voter (as in England) is a matter for some doubt. When there is a press of voters, the placing of the official mark, if done at the time of

the delivery of each ballot, is apt to be hurried, and its inadvertent omission may disfranchise an innocent voter. For this reason it was proposed in England, in 1876, to do away with the official mark, or to permit it to be placed in advance on all the ballots; but neither proposal was adopted. Probably the inconvenience in England largely resulted from the practice, already referred to, of requiring the presiding officer to distribute and to receive ballots at the same time. The danger of counterfeiting the design seems not to be greater under the Massachusetts method, for in either case the block must be prepared beforehand. Whatever the method followed, a stamp is better than the pencilled initials of the ballot clerk (as in S. Australia).

2. The numbered counterfoil system requires a few words. It is now in use in Great Britain, Ontario, W. Australia, and, in a simpler form, in Victoria. Its principal purpose is of course to be able to identify the ballot of any voter afterwards proved to have voted illegally or to have been bribed, and to discard his vote with certainty, saving, perhaps, the need of a new election. It is cumbrous, however, and tends to create errors, and the testimony in England, in 1876, was that its advantage was not great. The plan (in use in Queensland and New Zealand) of folding and gumming a corner of the ballot marked with the elector's number, is tedious and not satisfactory. It is a question whether, considering all things, the object is important enough to require these precautions.

3. To prevent what has been known as the "Tasmanian dodge," an ingenious device was adopted in Quebec (see Part VIII. G.), and subsequently by the Dominion Parliament, which checkmates what has often been supposed to be theoretically, if not practically, possible. The "Tasmanian dodge" (which appeared in Australia once only, in 1868, where it was immediately detected, and has apparently not been attempted in England), consists in sending in a voter who manages to deposit a counterfeit ballot (or empty envelope, if an envelope is required, as it should not be) and to bring out his own genuine one; which is then marked in ink by the local manager without, and given to another henchman, who in turn brings out a fresh ballot, and the process is repeated. In Quebec the election officer as he gives out the ballot, places on the back of a counterfoil or "annex" the voter's registered number; and when

the voter returns with the ballot marked, it is easy to see by comparing the number on the back of the "annex" with the registered number of the person presenting it, whether it is the same person to whom the ballot was delivered. The annex is then torn off and destroyed, and, while entire secrecy of voting is preserved, the Tasmanian dodge is effectually prevented, even in theory. This device merits a wider adoption.

NOTE 8.

Assistance to Illiterates and to others.

(Mass., § 25; S. Austr., § 58, VII.; Queens., § 73; Gt. Brit., B, § 26; Belg., § 123; Ky., § 10; N. Y., § 25.)

Assistance is allowed to illiterate electors in Great Britain, New York and Massachusetts, as well as in New Zealand, Canada, and Italy (Part VIII.). Where a reading and writing qualification does not exist, there can be no doubt that this is eminently just, and that if illiterates are to be disfranchised (as they should be) it may be done in a more straightforward way. Under the New York and Massachusetts laws the illiterate may select one of the election officers to assist him. It would seem that the presence of two officers, if possible, should be required; for as was found in England, attempts may be made to carry out bargains by pleading illiteracy and proving to the officer of the voter's party that the bargain is kept. Moreover, intimidation or fraud may occur if only one officer is present. It is better that in every case one officer of each party represented should be at hand. The publicity is no objection, for the voter's party is even more easily ascertained from his choice (if he is given it) of a single officer to assist him. In England, in 1876,[1] many returning officers wished the privilege of receiving assistance to be withdrawn, as subject to abuse, and the Committee so recommended; but it would seem that the objection of the officials arose largely from the cumbrous English provisions for reading and signing a long declaration of illiteracy. The verbal one permitted by the acts of this country seems sufficient. But a record should be kept, as it is in Great Britain, Belgium, and Kentucky, of all ballots marked with the assistance of the officers, whether for illiteracy, blindness, or any other cause.

[1] Parl. Papers, 1876, vol. xii.

Note 9.

Mode of Expressing the Vote.

(Mass., § 23; S Austr., § 58, VI.; Queens., § 73; Gt. Brit., A, § 2, B, § 25 C. " Form of Directions for Voters; " Belg., A, § 124, B, § 1; Ky., § 9; N. Y., § 22.)

Although this is one of the most interesting portions of the system, very little can be here said which will not suggest itself to those who examine the provisions of the different statutes. The two rival methods are that of striking out names not voted for, and that of marking a cross for the preferred candidates. The weak point (relatively) of the former is its tediousness, and of the latter is the opportunity offered for making the mark in other than the exact place and mode. Various plans are used for reducing this opportunity to a minimum. The best theoretical method is the Belgian, which leaves a small white spot for the voter to blacken; or perhaps the black ballot (proposed by Mr. Pearson of Stockport, Eng.) having white squares for the voter's mark.[1] Probably the best practical plan is that of the Dominion statute, all left-hand margin being discarded, and the upright line at the right being omitted. But it may be asserted that there is no real difficulty in the method, so far as ascertaining the elector's desire (which is the fundamental object of election proceedings) is concerned. The difficulties, if any, which have occurred with respect to this method of marking, have arisen, in the great majority of cases, solely from the provision in the British and Canadian statutes making void a ballot which contains " any mark by which the voter may afterwards be identified," which, in the hands of a few returning officers and many of the courts (especially in Scotland and in Canada)[2] has been applied in an unpractical and over-suspicious manner. It would be better to consider solely the voter's intention (which, as the testimony cited in the Introduction shows, seldom causes much difficulty), and to leave the question of collusion to be otherwise determined; perhaps, as a compromise measure, putting the burden

---

[1] Parl. Papers, 1876, vol. xii., app. to Report.

[2] The editor has already collected most of the material for an annotated edition, to be published before the fall elections, of the provisions common to the various statutes, including references to the decisions of the last thirty years in Great Britain, Ireland, Canada, and Australia.

on one who charges at the counting that a peculiar mark has been corruptly used, or, better still, as in the New York Act, imposing a penalty on one who marks collusively, but not placing upon the election officers the duty of entertaining the question, or allowing it to be raised at the counting of the votes. The construction of the ballots should continue to be governed by the present plain principle of election law that the voter's intention, whenever it clearly appears, should be given effect.

Note 10.

What Ballots shall not be Counted.

(Mass., § 26; S. Austr., § 64; Queens., § 76; Gt. Brit., A, § 2; Belg., §§ 124, 127; Ky., § 11; N. Y., §§ 13, 28.)

To the ordinary causes of rejection applicable to all ballots (*e. g.* that the vote is uncertain, because it is illegible or because too many names are voted for), it would seem that the present system should properly add but one cause peculiar to itself, — failure of the ballot to bear proof that it was lawfully received from and deposited with the officials of the election. In some statutes the absence of *prima facie* proof of this sort, in other words, the want of the official identifying mark, whatever it may be, justifies the rejection of the ballot (New York, *ubi supra*). In other statutes regard is paid to the actual, not merely the *prima facie* genuineness of the ballot; as in Massachusetts, where " none but the ballots provided in accordance with the provisions of this act shall be counted," that is (probably, though not clearly), all ballots actually provided by the Secretary, and actually received by the elector from the ballot clerk, must be counted. Between the two principles a choice must be made. The former, by fixing a definite test, gains in decisiveness and speed; the latter has the advantage of occasionally saving an honest vote from rejection.

The only other cause for rejection commonly sanctioned is the use of a collusive mark. As to the advisability of this provision an opinion has been already expressed (Note 9). It is not adopted in either the Kentucky, New York, or Massachusetts statutes.

Note 11.

Responsibility of Officials for Neglect of Duty.

(Mass., § 80; S. Austr., § 85; Queens., § 120; Gt. Brit., § 11; N. Y. § 31.)

That a general clause imposing a penalty upon an officer neglecting any duty placed upon him by the statute should be included therein seems unquestionable. Whether any provision should be made for abrogating or modifying the officer's responsibility in damages to one injured by his failure to perform the duty is a matter for some consideration. It seems that the duties of stamping the ballot, delivering it, receiving it, etc., are ministerial only (Pickering *v.* James, L. R. 8. C. P. 489; 55 L. T. 135; 11 Cent. L. J. 141), and that an officer is therefore at common law liable for any loss incurred through his failure, whether wilful or inadvertent, to perform such a duty. Provision, then, ought to be made for fixing a pecuniary limit to the civil liability of an officer, so that the maximum extent of his responsibility in case of loss might be known beforehand to himself and to all others concerned. To leave in force the common-law rule of indefinite responsibility, where the compensation of the position is comparatively a mere bagatelle, would be unjust, and would deter desirable men from accepting the duties. But care should be taken, in such a case, to make it clear (See Brett, J. in Pickering *v.* James, *supra*) that the statutory provision entirely supersedes the common law liability.

Note 12.

Informalities.

(S. Austr., § 71; Queens., § 85; Gt. Brit., A, § 13; Ky., § 26.)

It is perhaps advisable to insert a clause curing all informalities which do not affect the merits of the contest. This, however, would be extremely difficult to phrase properly, and had better be omitted than poorly done. The English provision has been more difficult to construe than it should have been, and is hardly a good model for a provision of similar purpose.

Note 13.

Objections to Nominations.

(Mass., § 7; Gt. Brit., B, § 13, D, § 8.)

In order to avoid the possibility of causing a new election upon trifling grounds, it is a great advantage to settle finally all questions relating to nominations before the election takes place. For this purpose a time and place are prescribed in the above statutes for making and hearing objections to the legality of nominations. The decisions of the tribunal are in Massachusetts final, in Great Britain are final only where an objection is held invalid. The former provision would perhaps in some places confer a dangerous power on an extra-judicial body.

Neither of the above statutes contains the very desirable proviso that, in case of the rejection of a nomination for non-fulfilment of the statutory requirements, if the defect is within a certain limited time repaired, the nomination may be again filed and shall then be treated as valid.[1]

Note 14.

Method of Reckoning Time.

(S. Austr., § 101; Gt. Brit., B, § 56; Ky., § 2.)

Framers of future statutes should not omit to declare whether Sundays are to be included in the computation of the periods for filing nominations, etc.; nor to make it entirely clear to what point the reckoner is carried by such provisions as "five days before the day of," or "five days at least before the day of" this or that event.

Note 15.

Deposit or Security from Candidates.

(Queens., §§ 49, 55; Gt. Brit., E; Ky., § 2.)

In Australia the object of the deposit — to discourage reckless candidacies — has already been commented on (Note 2.) In

---

[1] See the New York bill of 1880, Appendix I.

Great Britain, Canada, and Kentucky, it is a method of distributing the expense among the candidates. In this aspect it ought not to commend itself to those who are trying to escape from the evils of a machine corruption which rests largely on a similar system of assessments upon candidates. The cases are not entirely parallel, but the assessment of candidates, whether by the State or by a political committee, has many identical evils which will easily suggest themselves. We ought, moreover, to remember that in the Dominion elections the whole number of parliamentary candidates is seldom half a dozen, and the amount assessed being only $50 each, the sum collected is not intended to reimburse the election expenses of the district; while in England, where the security required from the candidates is much larger, the requirement is simply a part of the traditional system; the returning officer is personally liable for the expenses, and is not unlike an officially-appointed agent of the candidates, entitled to demand security in advance. In our own country, on the contrary, we have always recognized that, so far as the State takes electoral machinery into its own hands, to that extent it should undertake the expenses. In other words, the plan of imposing election expenses by law upon candidates proceeds upon the entirely false theory that it is the individual candidates, and not the people, for whose interests and needs the election was instituted. That this principle already finds support among a certain sordid few, to whom, as a recent writer has said, place-hunting is a career, makes it none the less unfortunate that it should be sanctioned in legislation. But upon whatever principle or theory the assessment of candidates may rest, perhaps the best reason for refusing to adopt it is, as has been said, that it savors too much of the very system of party assessments that we are now endeavoring to sweep away.

NOTE 16.

Space for Additional Names on Ballot.

(Mass., § 10; N. Y., § 13; Ky., § 9.)

A provision requiring space to be left, in the case of each office, for any additional name (or for as many as there are vacancies to be filled) that the elector may choose to insert, is essential to the complete theoretical fairness of the system; and the ballot can be arranged,[1] without inconvenience, so as to permit this.

Note 17.

Withdrawals.

(Mass., § 8; S. Austr., § 54; Gt. Brit., A, § 1, D, § 1 (7); N. Y., § 11.)

In none of the above statutes has a clause been inserted to provide against an important contingency, — the corrupt withdrawal of a candidate, in collusion with the opposite party or candidate. Without some such provision this becomes a vulnerable point in the system. Opportunities will frequently exist, with respect to candidates for many of the less prominent offices, at the last moment to make a "deal," to apply pressure, or even to purchase outright; and thus, with their candidate withdrawn and the time for nominations expired, the party or the section of electors is defeated even without an election.

This possibility may be easily obviated by allowing a day or two (after the expiration of the period for withdrawing) within which to substitute another candidate.

[1] See the model at the end of the book.

II. SOUTH AUSTRALIA.

ELECTORAL ACT, 1879 (42, 43 VICT., No. 141).

[PRELIMINARY (Sects. 1–4).]

[PART I. — APPOINTMENT OF OFFICERS, AND REGISTRATION (SECTS. 5–45).]

PART II. — CONDUCT OF ELECTIONS (SECTS. 46–71).

46, 47. (Form of election-writ; the polling day to be not less than two and not more than thirty days from the day of nomination.) (*a*)

(*a*) Mass., § 6; Queens., §§ 48, 49; Gt. Br. B, §§ 4, 14, D, § 1 (3); Belg., § 105; Ky., § 2; N. Y., § 8.

48. In order that any person may become or be a candidate at any election, he shall be nominated by not less than two persons (*b*) entitled to vote at such election, in manner following, that is to say, after the issue of the writ and before the time fixed for the nomination, there shall be delivered to the returning officer (*c*) a nomination paper, in the form, or to the effect of the form in the Tenth Schedule hereto, naming such person as a candidate at such election, and signed by the persons nominating as aforesaid, and having at the foot thereof a statement, under the hand of the person so nominated, that he consents to act if elected. (*c′*)

(*b*) Mass., § 4; Queens., § 49; Gt. Br., A, § 1; Belg., §§ 106, 155; Ky., § 2; N. Y., § 5; and NOTE 2, p. 53.

(*c*) Mass. § 6; Queens., § 49; Gt. Br., B, § 8, D, § 1 (3); Belg., § 106; Ky., § 2; N. Y., § 4.

49. (Publication by Returning Officer of dates of nomination and election and of polling-places.)

(*c′*) Belg., § 107; and NOTE 3, p. 54.

50. The Returning Officer shall at noon, on the day of nomination, attend at the chief polling-place, and there publicly produce the several nomination papers he shall

SOUTH AUSTRALIA.

have then received, and give notice (*d*) of the names of the persons nominated.

51. In case there shall be no greater number of candidates duly nominated than are required to be elected, the Returning Officer shall declare such candidate or candidates to be elected, and make his return accordingly.

52. In case more such candidates shall be duly nominated, the Returning Officer shall give notice thereof (*d*), of the names of the candidates, and of the day and time of taking the poll.

53. (Polling-booths to be provided, and poll-clerks and doorkeepers to be appointed.)

54. Each polling-booth shall have separate compartments (*e*), and shall be provided with a ballot-box having an inner cover, with a cleft therein, for receiving the voting papers, and a lock and key, and an outer cover with a lock and key; and the said compartments shall be constructed so as to screen any voter therein from observation, and shall be furnished with pencils for the use of voters.

55. The Returning Officer shall cause voting papers to be printed which shall contain the Christian and surnames of the several candidates arranged (*f*) in alphabetical order according to such surnames; and if there are two candidates of the same surname, then according to the Christian name of such candidates; and if there are two candidates of the same Christian name and surname, then according to the residences of such candidates, arranged in the like order, and a square printed opposite the name of each candidate, and he shall obtain a sufficient number (*g*) of voting papers.

56. Before the hour of polling the Returning Officer shall deliver to the substitutes at each polling-booth a list of the electors on the said roll who have been registered for six months, and who claim to vote at such polling-booth, herein called "list of voters," together with a copy or copies of the roll in force for the division or district, as the case may be, for use at the said polling, and shall sign

(*d*) Mass., §§ 14, 15; Queens., §§ 50, 53; Gt. Br., B, § 9, D, 1 (3); Belg., § 112; Ky., § 5; N. Y., § 10.

(*e*) Mass., § 21; Queens., § 59; Gt. Br., B, § 16; Belg., § 117; Ky., § 8; N.Y., § 20; and Note 5, p. 58.

(*f*) Mass., § 10; Queens., § 58; Gt. Br., B, § 22, D, § 1 (6); Belg., §§ 114, 115; Ky., § 4; N.Y., § 14; and Note 4, p. 58.

(*g*) Mass., § 12; Queens., § 58; Ky., § 3; N. Y., § 16; *infra*, § 56.

each page of such list; and shall also deliver to each substitute, and himself retain such numbers respectively of the voting-papers as shall be sufficient (*h*) for the use of the electors at such booth.

(h) See § 55, *ante*, note *(g)*.

57. Before delivering the voting papers to the electors, each Returning Officer, or his substitute, shall initial (*i*) such papers on the face thereof, and fold them, and keep an exact account of all initialled voting papers.

(i) Mass., § 10; Queens., § 71; Gt. Br., A, § 2, B, § 24; Belg., §§ 123, 151; Ky., §§ 4, 7; N.Y., § 21; and NOTE 7, p. 50.

58. On the day of election the poll shall be taken at the several polling-places according to the following regulations:—

I. (Hours of opening; care of the ballot-box.)

II. (Hours of closing.)

III. Every person proposing to vote shall state to the presiding officer, or to some one of his clerks, his Christian name and surname, and if so required any other of the particulars, necessary to be expressed in the roll, which the said officer may require for the sole purpose of enabling him to ascertain the name upon the roll intended by such person.

(j) Mass., § 22; Queens., § 71; Gt. Br., B, § 50; Belg., § 123; Ky., § 7; N.Y., § 21; and NOTE 6, p. 59.

IV. The presiding officer or voting clerk (*j*) shall ascertain if the name intended by the voter is upon the list of voters; and if so found he shall, subject as hereafter provided, deliver to such voter a voting paper bearing the initials of the Returning Officer, or his substitute, and shall place a mark against the voter's name on the list of voters.

V. If a person representing himself to be a particular elector named on the roll applies for a voting paper after another person has voted as such elector, the applicant shall, upon duly answering the questions in the Eleventh Schedule, be entitled to receive a voting paper in the same manner as any other voter.

VI. The voter shall forthwith retire alone to some unoccupied compartment of the said booth, and shall there in private, and without delay, indicate the name of each candidate for whom he intends to vote by (*k*) making a cross, the centre of which cross shall be contained within

(k) Mass., § 23; Queens., § 73;

the square opposite the name of such candidate, and shall then fold the voting paper, and immediately deliver it so folded to the presiding officer, who shall openly forthwith, and without unfolding the same, deposit it in the ballot-box; and the voter shall then quit the polling-booth. Gt. Br., A, § 2, B, § 25, C, "Form of Directions for Voters;" Belg., A, § 124, B, § 1; Ky., § 9; N.Y., § 22; and Note 9, p. 62.

VII. Any voter may signify to the presiding officer that by reason of blindness (*l*) he is unable to comply with the last preceding regulation; and thereupon the presiding officer, if satisfied that such voter is afflicted with blindness, shall permit any agent named by such voter to accompany him into the compartment set apart for the purpose, to mark the voting paper on such voter's behalf, and hand the same to the Returning Officer, who shall deposit the same in the ballot-box. (*l*) Mass., § 25; Queens., § 73; Gt. Br., B, § 23; Belg., § 123; Ky., § 10; N.Y., § 25; and Note 8, p. 61.

VIII. Any person who, by mistake or accident, shall spoil (*m*) any voting paper, may, before the same shall have been deposited in the ballot-box, upon signifying the same to the Returning Officer and delivering up the spoiled voting paper, obtain a fresh voting paper; and the spoiled voting paper shall be then and there destroyed by burning the same. (*m*) Mass., § 24; Gt. Br., B, § 28; Belg., § 125; Ky., § 9; N.Y., § 24.

IX. (Provision for closing and sealing the ballot-box.)

59. The Returning Officer (or his substitute), the poll clerks, and doorkeepers and scrutineers (not exceeding two for each candidate, to be appointed in writing), and electors about to vote, shall alone (*n*) be permitted at any one time, without the consent of the Returning Officer or his substitute, to enter or remain in the polling-booth during the taking of the poll. (*n*) Mass., § 21; Queens., § 59; Gt. Br., B, § 21; Belg., § 97; Ky., § 17; N.Y., § 20; and Note 1, p. 52.

60. (Questions to voters as to qualifications, etc.)

61. If the person so proposing to vote shall refuse to answer any question or shall answer the same in such manner as to show that he is not qualified to vote, he shall not be permitted to vote, and he shall forthwith return to the presiding officer the voting paper, if any, delivered to him, and which paper shall thereupon be immediately destroyed by the said presiding officer.

62. (Ballot-boxes to be delivered to the respective Returning Officers.)

63. All voting papers issued to any substitute, and not used by him, and all lists of voters, shall be returned by him to the Returning Officer, with the ballot-box.

64. (Proceedings relative to the counting of the voting papers.)

(o) Mass., § 26; Queens., § 76; Gt. Br., A, § 2; Belg., §§ 124, 147; Ky., § 11; N. Y., §§ 13, 28; and NOTE 10, p. 63.

... The Returning Officer shall reject (o) all voting papers not initialled, or which shall contain crosses against the names of a larger number of candidates than are required to be elected, or shall contain anything marked or written other than the initials of the Returning Officer or his substitute and the cross indicating the name of such candidate for whom the elector intends to vote. . . .

67. The Returning Officer of the district shall send to the Returning Officer of the province, a return, in a tabular form, of the number of electors on the roll, the number of voting papers found in the ballot-boxes, the number of voting papers allowed, the number of voting papers rejected, distinguishing the number, 1st, not initialled by the Returning Officer or his substitute; 2d, voting for more candidates than entitled to be elected; 3d, containing writing or marks by which the voter can be identified; 4th, unmarked or informally marked voting papers.

(p) Queens., § 85; Gt. Br., A, § 13; Ky., § 26; and NOTE 12, p. 64.

71. No election shall be held to be void (p) in consequence solely of . . . any error on the part of any Returning Officer or deputy, which shall not affect the result of the election, or of any error or impediment of a mere formal nature. . . .

PART III. — OFFENCES AND PENALTIES (SECTS. 72–86).

72. Every person who —

I. Forges or fraudulently defaces or fraudulently destroys any nomination paper, or delivers to the Returning Officer any nomination paper, knowing the same to be forged; or

II. Forges or counterfeits or fraudulently defaces, or

fraudulently destroys any voting paper or the initials on any voting paper; or

III. Without due authority supplies any voting paper to any person; or

IV. Fraudulently puts into any ballot-box any paper other than the voting paper which he is authorized by law to put in; or

V. Fraudulently takes out of the polling-booth any voting paper; or

VI. Without due authority destroys, takes, opens, or otherwise interferes with any ballot-box or voting papers then in use for the purposes of the election; or

VII. Refuses to deliver to the Returning Officer or his substitute any voting paper in his possession, whether he shall have obtained such voting paper for the purpose of recording his vote or not, —

Shall be guilty of a misdemeanor, and be liable, if he is a Returning Officer, or an officer or clerk in attendance at a polling-booth, to imprisonment for any term not exceeding two years, with or without hard labor; and, if he is any other person, to imprisonment for any term not exceeding six months, with or without hard labor; and any attempt to commit any offence specified in this section shall be punishable in the manner in which the offence itself is punishable.

73. In any indictment or other prosecution for an offence in relation to the nomination papers, ballot-boxes, and voting papers at an election, the property in such papers and boxes may be stated to be in the Returning Officer at such election.

85. If any Returning Officer for the said province, or any District Returning Officer, after having accepted office as such, shall neglect or refuse to perform (*q*) any of the duties which by the provisions hereof he is required to perform, every such Returning Officer or District Returning Officer shall, for every such offence, forfeit any sum not less than Ten nor exceeding Two Hundred Pounds, and in like manner if any substitute, clerk, or other officer

(*q*) Mass., § 30; Queens., § 120; Gt. Br., A, § 11; N. Y., § 31; and Note 11, p. 64.

or person appointed or required to perform any duty, under or by virtue of this act, shall neglect or refuse to perform (*q*) any of the duties which by the provisions hereof he is required to perform, every such clerk or other officer or person shall, for every such offence, forfeit and pay any sum not less than Five and not exceeding Fifty Pounds.

[PART IV.— COURT FOR THE TRIAL OF DISPUTED RETURNS (SECTS. 87–100).]

PART V. — GENERAL MATTERS (SECTS. 101–106).

(*r*)
Gt. Br., B, § 56;
Ky., § 2; and
NOTE 14, p. 65.

101. When any matter or thing is hereby directed to be performed on a certain day, and that day shall happen to be a Sunday, Good Friday, Christmas Day, or other public holiday, the said matter or thing may be performed on the next succeeding day, not being any of the days aforesaid (*r*).

III. QUEENSLAND.

ELECTIONS ACT, 1885 (49 VICT. No. 13).

[PART I. — DEFINITIONS AND PRELIMINARY MATTER (SECTS. 1–5).]

[PART II. — QUALIFICATIONS OF ELECTORS (SECTS. 6–8).]

[PART III. — REGISTRATION (SECTS. 9–43).]

PART IV. — ELECTION WRITS AND OFFICERS; NOMINATIONS AND CONDUCT OF ELECTIONS (SECTS. 44–78.)

Election Officers (Sects. 44–46).

45. Every person appointed a returning officer, presiding officer, or poll clerk under this Act, shall before he enters on the duties of such office, make and subscribe a solemn declaration before some justice in the following form: —

I, A. B., do hereby declare that I accept the office of Returning Officer [*or* Presiding Officer at   , *or* Poll Clerk, *as the case may be*] for the Electoral District of   , and I hereby promise and declare that I will faithfully perform the duties of my office to the best of my understanding and ability, and that I will not attempt to improperly ascertain or discover, or by any word or action directly or indirectly aid in discovering the person for whom any vote is given. And that I will keep secret all knowledge of the person for whom any elector has voted which I may obtain in the exercise of my office, unless in answer to any question which I am legally bound to answer.

A. B.

Declared before me this }
   day of   , 18 . }

        C. D ——, J. P.

And such justice shall transmit the declaration so made by the first convenient opportunity to the Colonial Secretary.

Writs (Sects. 47, 48).

48. The returning officer shall endorse upon the writ so directed to him the day on which he receives it, and shall forthwith give public notice of the day and place of nomination, and of the day of polling mentioned in the writ, and of the several polling-places, and of a convenient house or place within the electoral district, to be named by the returning officer, as the place of nomination at which he will be present between the hours of four and six o'clock after noon on the day preceding the day of nomination for the purpose of receiving the nomination papers of candidates, and shall also as soon as possible give public notice of any polling-place appointed after the issue of the writ.

Provided that a nomination paper may be received by the returning officer at any time or place before the said hour of four o'clock (*a*).

Nominations (Sects. 49–55).

49. In order that any person may be or become a candidate at an election, he shall be nominated by not less than six persons (*b*) entitled to vote at such election, in manner following, that is to say, before six o'clock after noon of the day preceding the day of nomination named in the writ (*d*), there shall be delivered to the returning officer (*e*), who shall if required give a receipt for the same, a nomination-paper naming such person as a candidate at such election and signed by the persons nominating him in the following form : —

(*a*) See § 48, *infra*, note (*c*).

(*b*) Mass., § 4; S. Austr., § 48; Gt. Br., A. § 1; Belg., §§ 106, 155; Ky., § 2; N. Y., § 5; and Note 2, p. 53.

(*d*) *Ante*, § 48; Mass., § 6; S. Austr., § 46; Gt. Br., B, §§ 4, 14, D, § 1 (3); Belg., § 105; Ky., § 2; N. Y., § 8.

(*e*) Mass., § 6; S. Austr., § 48; Gt. Br., B, § 8, D, § 1 (3); Belg., § 106; Ky., § 2; N. Y. § 4.

QUEENSLAND. 77

We, the undersigned electors of the Electoral District of ,
do hereby nominate [*state Christian name and surname*] of
[*state residence and occupation*] for the office of member of
the Legislative Assembly for the said district in pursuance of a
writ of election issued the   day of   18 .
   Dated this   day of   , 18 .
              [*Here are to follow the signatures.*]

And such person or some person in his behalf shall, at
the time of delivery of such nomination-paper, pay (*f*) to
the returning officer in sterling money or bank notes the
sum of twenty pounds, to be dealt with as hereinafter provided; and no person who is not so nominated, or by or for
whom or on whose behalf such payment is not made, shall
be or be deemed to be, a candidate at the election.

(*f*)
Infra, § 55;
Gt. Br., E;
Ky., § 2; and
Note 15, p. 65.

50. Immediately on the receipt of a nomination-paper it
shall be the duty of the returning officer to post (*g*) a copy
thereof outside the nearest police office, or if there is no
police office at the place of nomination, then in some conspicuous place there.

(*g*)
See § 53, *infra*,
note (*h*).

51. (Uncertificated insolvent incapable of nomination or
election.)

52. If the number of persons who are duly nominated
as candidates at any election does not exceed the number
of members to be elected, the returning officer shall, at
noon on the day of nomination at the place named as
aforesaid for the delivery of the nomination papers, publicly declare such candidates to be duly elected, and make
his return accordingly.

53. If the number of persons who are duly nominated
as candidates at any election exceeds the number of members to be elected, then for deciding between such candidates a poll shall take place on the day named in the writ
for that purpose at the several polling places for the district, and the returning officer shall, at noon on the day
and at the place named as aforesaid for the delivery of the
nomination-papers, publicly announce (*h*) the names of the
persons who have been duly nominated as candidates, and
that a poll will be so taken, and shall also forthwith pub-

(*h*)
Mass., §§ 14,
15;
S. Austr., § 50;

lish (*h*) the like announcement in some newspaper published in the district or, if none such is published, then in the newspaper published nearest to the district.

<small>Gt. Br., B, § 9,
D, § 1 (3);
Belg., § 112;
Ky., § 5;
N. Y., § 10.</small>

54. If any candidate is desirous of retiring (*i*) from his candidature, he may, not later than two clear days after the day of nomination, sign and deliver to the returning officer a notice in the following form, or to the like effect: —

<small>(*i*)
Mass., § 8;
Gt. Br., A, § 1,
D, § 1 (7);
N. Y. § 11.</small>

To the Returning Officer of the Electoral District of   .

I, A. B., do hereby retire from being a candidate for election for the Electoral District of   at the ensuing election.

Dated this   day of   . 18 .

                (Signed)   A. B.

Witness   C. D.

The returning officer on the receipt of such notice shall omit the name of the person so retiring from the ballot papers to be used at the election, or, if any of such papers have been printed, shall erase his name therefrom. The person so retiring shall not be capable of being elected at the election. (Provision for declaring the remaining candidates elected without a poll, as in § 52, in case their number does not exceed the number to be elected.)

55. (Provision for returning to each candidate retiring, or declared elected without a poll, or receiving at least one fifth of the number of votes obtained by the successful candidate having the smallest number of votes, the sum advanced by him at the time of nomination (*j*).)

<small>(*j*)
See § 49, *ante*, note (f).</small>

Poll (Sects. 55–78).

56. For taking the poll at an election, the returning officer shall cause booths to be erected or rooms to be hired and used as such booths in one place at each polling-place as occasion may require.

57. (Provision for appointment by the returning officer of a presiding officer and one or more poll-clerks for each polling-place.)

58. Forthwith after a poll stands appointed for any election, the returning officer shall cause to be printed or written ballot papers containing the candidates' names in alphabetical order, and nothing else, according to the following form (*k*) : —

> JOHN DOE.
> RICHARD ROE.
> JAMES SMITH.
> HENRY THOMPSON.

(*k*) Mass., § 10; S. Austr., § 55; Gt. Br., B. § 22, D, § 1 (6); Belg., §§ 114, 115; Ky., § 4; N. Y., § 14; and NOTE 4, p. 55.

and shall supply to the presiding officer of each polling-place so many of such ballot papers as shall be fully equal to the number of electors likely to vote at such polling-place (*l*), and shall keep for himself a like sufficient number for the polling-place at which he is to preside. If two candidates have the same Christian name and surname, the residence and description of each candidate shall be added to his name on the ballot paper.

(*l*) Mass., § 12; S. Austr., § 56; Ky., § 3; N. Y., § 16.

59. At every booth or polling-place there shall be one or more compartment or compartments (*m*) provided with all necessary materials for the purpose of enabling the electors to mark the ballot papers as hereinafter provided, and in such booth or polling-place no person shall be entitled to be present (*n*) other than the presiding officer, the poll-clerk, the candidates, and the scrutineers of the several candidates to be appointed as hereinafter provided, and the electors who for the time are voting.

The presiding officer or poll-clerk may summon to his assistance in such booth or polling-place any member of the police force for the purpose of preserving the public peace or preventing any breach thereof, and for removing out of such booth or polling-place any person who in his opinion is obstructing the polling or wilfully violating any of the provisions of this Act.

(*m*) Mass., § 21; S. Austr., § 54; Gt. Br., B. § 16; Belg., § 118; Ky., § 8; N. Y., § 20; and NOTE 5, p. 58.

(*n*) Mass., § 21; S. Austr., § 59; Gt. Br., B, § 21; Belg., § 97; Ky., § 17; N. Y., § 20; and NOTE 1, p. 52.

60. (The presiding officer shall furnish a ballot-box, which shall be examined before the balloting begins.)

61. (The polls are to open at 8 o'clock and close at 4 o'clock, except under certain circumstances.)

62. (Provision in detail for the appointment and qualification of candidates' scrutineers for each polling-place.)

63–70. (Interrogations and oaths as to qualifications, etc., for persons claiming to be entitled to vote.)

71. When an elector has satisfied the presiding officer that he is entitled to vote at the election, the presiding officer (*o*) shall deliver to him a ballot paper. Before delivery of the ballot paper to the elector the presiding officer shall mark (*p*) the same on the face thereof with his initials in ink or pencil, and shall also write (*p*) upon the back of the left-hand upper corner of the ballot paper in ink or pencil the number set against the name of the elector in the electoral roll.

The presiding officer shall then, and before delivery of the ballot paper to the elector, fold down (*p*) the corner of the paper so as to entirely conceal the number so written, and shall securely fasten the fold with gum or otherwise in such a manner that the number cannot be discovered without unfastening the fold.

(o)
Mass., § 22;
S. Austr., § 58,
IV.;
Gt. Br., B. § 50;
Belg., § 123;
Ky., § 7;
N. Y., § 21;
and Note 6,
p. 59.

(p)
Mass., § 10;
S. Austr., § 57;
Gt. Br., A., § 2, B., § 24;
Belg., §§ 123, 151;
Ky., § 417;
N. Y., § 21;
and Note 7,
p. 59.

72. Upon delivery of the ballot paper to the elector, the presiding officer or poll-clerk shall, upon the copy of the electoral roll in use by him, or, in the case of a presiding officer other than the returning officer, upon the certified copy of the roll supplied to him by the returning officer, make a mark against the name of the elector. The mark so made on the roll shall be *prima facie* evidence of the identity of the person to whom the ballot paper is delivered with the elector whose name is so marked on the roll, and of the fact that such elector voted at that election.

The number marked upon the back of the ballot paper shall, upon a scrutiny, be conclusive evidence that such ballot-paper was delivered to and used by the person who claimed to vote as the person against whose name such number is set in the electoral roll.

73. The elector, having received a ballot paper, shall, in one of the compartments or ballot rooms provided for the

purpose, strike out (*q*) from his ballot paper the names of such candidates as he does not intend to vote for, and shall make no other mark or writing thereon, and shall forthwith fold up the paper in such manner as will conceal the names of the candidates, and deposit it in the ballot-box in the presence of the presiding officer. Provided that while an elector is in a compartment preparing his ballot paper no other person shall be allowed in such compartment. Provided, nevertheless, that in case any elector is unable to read, or is blind (*r*), he shall signify the fact to the presiding officer, who shall thereupon, in the booth or polling-place, and in the presence and sight of the poll-clerks, candidates, and scrutineers, strike out the names of the candidate or candidates other than the candidate or candidates for whom the elector says that he desires to vote.

(*q*) Mass., § 23; S. Austr., § 58, VI.; Gt. Br., A., § 2, B, § 25, C, "Form of Directions for Voters"; Belg., A, § 124. B, § 1; Ky., § 9; N. Y., § 22; and NOTE 9, p. 62.

(*r*) Mass., § 25; S. Austr., § 58, VII.; Gt. Br., B, § 26; Belg., § 123; Ky., § 10; N. Y., § 25; and NOTE 8, p. 61.

No elector shall take out of the booth or polling-place any ballot paper either before or after the same has been so marked.

Any elector wilfully infringing any of the provisions of this section, or obstructing the polling by any unnecessary delay in performing any act within the ballot room, shall be guilty of a misdemeanor.

74. (Provisions for disposing of second votes tendered on the same name.)

75. An elector may vote for any number of candidates not exceeding the number of members then to be elected.

76. Every ballot paper which (*s*) —
 (1) Does not bear the initials of the presiding officer, or,
 (2) Does not appear to have the elector's number written upon the back of it by the presiding officer as hereinbefore provided, or
 (3) Has such number torn off, or
 (4) Contains a greater number of names of candidates not struck out than the number of members to be elected, or

(*s*) Mass., § 26; S. Austr., § 64; Gt. Br., A, § 2; Belg., §§ 124, 147; Ky., § 11; N. Y., §§ 13, 28; and NOTE 10, p. 63.

(5) Has upon it any mark or writing not by this Act authorized to be put thereon,

shall be rejected at the close of the poll.

77. (Provision for adjournment in case of a riot.)

78. (Power given to the presiding officer to maintain order.)

Part V. — Declaration of the Result, and Return of Writs of Election (Sects. 79–87).

<small>(*t*)
S. Austr., § 71;
Gt. Br., A, § 13;
Ky., § 26;
and Note 12,
p. 64.</small>

85. No election under this Act shall be liable to be questioned (*t*) by reason of any defect in the title, or any want of title, of any person by or before whom such election is held, if such person really acted at such election, nor by reason of any formal error or defect in any declaration or other instrument, or in any publication made under this Act or intended to be so made, nor by reason of any such publication being out of time.

87. All expenses which a returning officer necessarily incurs in and about an election under the provisions of this Act shall be defrayed out of such moneys as shall be appropriated by Parliament for that purpose.

Part VI. — Corrupt and Illegal Practices (Sects. 88–110).

95 . . . (2). Any person who, before or during an election, knowingly publishes a false statement of the withdrawal of a candidate at such election for the purpose of promoting or procuring the election of another candidate, shall be guilty of an illegal practice.

99. Every person who corruptly induces or procures any other person to withdraw from being a candidate at an election, in consideration of any payment or promise of payment, and every person who withdraws in pursuance of such inducement or procurement, shall be guilty of illegal payment.

100. Every bill, placard, or poster having reference to an election shall bear upon the face thereof the name and

address of the printer and publisher thereof; and every person who prints, publishes, or posts, or causes to be printed, published, or posted, any such bill, placard, or poster, as aforesaid, which fails to bear upon the face thereof the name and address of the printer and publisher, shall, if he is the candidate, or the agent of the candidate, be guilty of an illegal practice; and if he is not the candidate, or the agent of a candidate, shall be liable on summary conviction to a fine not exceeding one hundred pounds.

PART VII. — SUPPLEMENTAL PROVISIONS (SECTS. 111-126).

116. Every person who intrudes into any booth or polling-place, other than the presiding officer, poll-clerk, candidates, scrutineers, and electors actually voting, shall be guilty of a misdemeanor.

120 ... (2). Every justice, presiding officer, or other officer or person who wilfully neglects or refuses to perform (*u*) any of the duties which by the provisions of this Act he is required to perform, shall for every such offence forfeit and pay any sum not exceeding fifty pounds.

(*u*) Mass., § 30; S. Austr., § 85; Gt. Br. A, § 11; N. Y., § 31; and NOTE 11, p. 64.

121. Every presiding officer or other person who places or is privy to placing in a ballot-box a ballot paper which has not been lawfully handed to and marked by an elector shall be guilty of felony, and shall be liable on conviction to be kept in penal servitude for any period not exceeding seven years, and not less than two years, or to be imprisoned for any term not exceeding two years, with or without hard labor. Proof that a greater number of ballot papers is found in a ballot-box, or is returned by a presiding officer as having been received at a polling-place, than the number of electors who voted at such polling-place, shall be *prima facie* evidence that the presiding officer at such polling-place was guilty of an offence against this section.

124 (1). Every returning officer, presiding officer, poll-clerk, scrutineer, or other person who knowingly and wilfully unfastens the fold upon a ballot paper within which

the number of an elector is written, unless he is by the lawful command of some competent court or other tribunal required to do so; and, —

(2). Every returning officer, presiding officer, poll-clerk, or scrutineer who attempts to ascertain or discover, or directly or indirectly aids in ascertaining or discovering, the person for whom any vote is given, except in the case of a person voting openly, or who, having in the exercise of his office obtained knowledge of the person for whom any elector has voted, discloses such knowledge, unless in answer to some question put in the course of proceedings before some competent court or other tribunal; and, —

(3). Every returning officer, presiding officer, poll-clerk, or scrutineer who places upon any ballot paper any mark or writing not authorized by this act,

Shall be guilty of a misdemeanor, and on conviction thereof shall be liable to imprisonment for any term not exceeding two years, with or without hard labor.

[PART VIII. — TEMPORARY PROVISIONS (SECTS. 127–131).]

IV.—GREAT BRITAIN AND IRELAND.

A. *Ballot Act,* 1872.
B. *First Schedule.*
C. *Second Schedule* (including forms for nomination and ballot papers).
D. *Municipal Elections Act,* 1875 (sect. 1, subs. 3, 6, 7).
E. *Parliamentary Elections (Returning Officers) Act,* 1875.

A.

BALLOT ACT, 1872 (35 and 36 VICT., C. 33).

PART I.— PARLIAMENTARY ELECTIONS.

Procedure at Elections.

1. A candidate for election to serve in Parliament for a county or borough, shall be nominated in writing. The writing shall be subscribed by two registered electors of such county or borough as proposer and seconder, and by eight other registered electors of the same county or borough as assenting to the nomination (*a*), and shall be delivered during the time appointed for the election to the returning officer by the candidate himself or his proposer or seconder.

If at the expiration of one hour after the time appointed for the election, no more candidates stand nominated than there are vacancies to be filled up, the returning officer shall forthwith declare the candidates who may stand nominated to be elected, and return their names to the clerk of the crown in chancery; but if at the expiration of such hour more candidates stand nominated than there are

(*a*) Mass., § 4; S. Austr., § 48; Queens., § 49; Belg., §§ 100, 155; Ky., § 2; N. Y., § 5; and NOTE 2, p. 53.

vacancies to be filled up, the returning officer shall adjourn the election and shall take a poll in manner in this Act mentioned.

(b)
Mass., § 8;
Queens., § 54;
N. Y., § 11;
Gt. Br., D, § 1
(7), infra.

A candidate may, during the time appointed for the election, but not afterwards, withdraw (b) from his candidature by giving a notice to that effect, signed by him, to the returning officer; provided, that the proposer of a candidate nominated in his absence out of the United Kingdom, may withdraw such candidate by a written notice signed by him and delivered to the returning officer, together with a written declaration of such absence of the candidate.

(Provision for proclaiming the election anew in case of the death of a candidate after nomination and before election.)

2. In the case of a poll at an election the votes shall be given by ballot. The ballot of each voter shall consist of a paper (in this Act called a ballot paper) showing the names and description of the candidates. Each ballot

(c)
Mass., § 10;
S. Austr., § 57;
Queens., § 71;
Belg., §§ 123, 151;
Ky., §§ 4, 7;
N. Y., § 21;
Gt. Br., B, § 24,
infra; and
NOTE 7, p. 59.

paper shall have (c) a number printed on the back, and shall have attached a counterfoil with the same number printed on the face. At the time of voting, the ballot paper shall be marked on both sides with an official mark, and delivered to the voter within the polling-station, and the number of such voter on the register of voters shall be marked on the counterfoil, and the voter, having secretly

(d)
Mass., § 23;
S. Austr., § 58,
VI.;
Queens., § 73;
Belg., A, § 124,
B, § 1;
Ky., § 9;
N. Y., § 22;
Gt. Br., B, § 25,
C, "Form of Directions for voters," infra; and NOTE 9, p. 62.

marked (d) his vote on the paper, and folded it up so as to conceal his vote, shall place it in a closed box in the presence of the officer presiding at the polling-station (in this Act called "the presiding officer") after having shown to him the official mark at the back.

Any ballot paper which has not on its back the official mark, or on which votes are given to more candidates than the voter is entitled to vote for, or on which anything, except the said number on the back, is written or marked, by which the voter can be identified, shall be void (e) and not counted.

(e)
Mass., § 26;
S. Austr., § 64;
Queens., § 76;

After the close of the poll the ballot-boxes shall be

sealed up, so as to prevent the introduction of additional ballot papers, and shall be taken charge of by the returning officer, and that officer shall, in the presence of such agents, if any, of the candidates as may be in attendance, open the ballot-boxes and ascertain the result of the poll by counting the votes given to each candidate, and shall forthwith declare to be elected the candidate or candidates to whom the majority of votes have been given, and return their names to the clerk of the crown in chancery. Belg., §§ 124, 147; Ky., § 11; N. Y., §§ 13, 28; and Note 10, p. 63.

The decision of the returning officer as to any question arising in respect of any ballot paper shall be final, subject to reversal on petition questioning the election or return (e'). (e') See note (k), *infra*.

(Provision for the casting of a vote by the returning officer only in case of a tie between two candidates.)

Offences at Elections.

3. Every person who —

(1) Forges or fraudulently defaces or fraudulently destroys any nomination paper, or delivers to the returning officer any nomination paper, knowing the same to be forged ; or

(2) Forges or counterfeits or fraudulently defaces or fraudulently destroys any ballot paper or the official mark on any ballot paper ; or

(3) Without due authority supplies any ballot paper to any person ; or

(4) Fraudulently puts into any ballot-box any paper other than the ballot paper which he is authorized by law to put in ; or

(5) Fraudulently takes out of the polling-station any ballot paper ; or

(6) Without due authority destroys, takes, opens, or otherwise interferes with any ballot-box or packet of ballot papers then in use for the purposes of the election,

shall be guilty of a misdemeanor, and be liable, if he is a returning officer or an officer or clerk in attendance at a polling-station, to imprisonment for any term not exceeding two years, with or without hard labor, and if he is any other person, to imprisonment for any term not exceeding six months, with or without hard labor.

Any attempt to commit any offence specified in this section shall be punishable in the manner in which the offence itself is punishable.

In any indictment or other prosecution for an offence in relation to the nomination papers, ballot-boxes, ballot papers, and marking-instruments at an election, the property in such papers, boxes, and instruments may be stated to be in the returning officer at such election, as well as the property in the counterfoils.

4. Every officer, clerk, and agent in attendance at a polling-station shall maintain, and aid in maintaining, the secrecy of the voting in such station, and shall not communicate, except for some purpose authorized by law, before the poll is closed, to any person, any information as to the name or number on the register of voters of any elector who has or has not applied for a ballot paper or voted at that station, or as to the official mark; and no such officer, clerk, or agent, and no person whosoever shall interfere with, or attempt to interfere with, a voter when marking his vote, or otherwise attempt to obtain in the polling-station information as to the candidate for whom any voter in such station is about to vote or has voted, or communicate at any time to any person any information obtained in a polling-station as to the candidate for whom any voter in such station is about to vote or has voted, or as to the number on the back of the ballot paper given to any voter at such station. Every officer, clerk, and agent in attendance at the counting of the votes shall maintain, and aid in maintaining, the secrecy of the voting, and shall not attempt to ascertain at such counting the number on the back of any ballot paper, or communicate any information obtained at such counting as to the candidate for whom any vote is given in any particular ballot paper. No person shall, directly or in-

GREAT BRITAIN AND IRELAND. 89

directly, induce any voter to display his ballot paper after he shall have marked the same, so as to make known to any person the name of the candidate for or against whom he has so marked his vote.

Every person who acts in contravention of the provisions of this section shall be liable, on summary conviction before two justices of the peace, to imprisonment for any term not exceeding six months, with or without hard labor.

5–7. (Division of counties and boroughs into polling-districts.)

Duties of Election Officers.

8. Subject to the provisions of this Act, every returning officer shall provide such nomination papers, polling-stations, ballot-boxes, ballot papers, stamping-instruments, copies of register of voters, and other things, appoint and pay such officers, and do such other acts and things as may be necessary for effectually conducting an election in manner provided by this Act.

All expenses properly incurred by any returning officer in carrying into effect the provisions of this Act, in the case of any parliamentary election, shall be payable in the same manner as expenses incurred in the erection of polling-booths at such election are by law payable.

(The sheriff in some instances may act as returning officer.)

9. (The presiding officer is empowered to keep order in the polling-station.)

10. (Election officers are empowered to ask the questions and administer the oaths authorized by law.)

11. Every returning officer, presiding officer, and clerk who is guilty of any wilful misfeasance, or any wilful act or omission in contravention of this Act shall, in addition to any other penalty or liability to which he may be subject, forfeit to any person aggrieved by such misfeasance, act, or omission, a penal sum not exceeding one hundred pounds (*f*).

(*f*) Mass., § 30; S. Austr., § 85; Queens., § 120; N. Y., § 31; and NOTE 11, p. 64.

(No election officer shall act as election agent for any candidate.)

Miscellaneous.

12. (No person shall be required to disclose his vote.)

13. No election shall be declared invalid by reason of a non-compliance with the rules contained in the first schedule to this Act, or any mistake in the use of the forms in the second schedule to this Act, if it appears to the tribunal having cognizance of the question that the election was conducted in accordance with the principles laid down in the body of this Act, and that such non-compliance or mistake did not affect the result of the election (*g*).

<small>(*g*)
S. Austr., § 71;
Queens., § 85;
Ky., § 26;
and NOTE 12, p. 64.</small>

14–20. (Miscellaneous provisions as to the construction of other Acts, and the application of this Act to Ireland and Scotland.)

PART II. — MUNICIPAL ELECTIONS.

20–23. (Application of the Act to municipal elections.)

PART III. — PERSONATION.

24–27. (Provisions relating to the offence of personation.)

PART IV.

(Miscellaneous provisions relating to repeals, etc.)

B.

FIRST SCHEDULE.

PART I. — Rules for Parliamentary Elections.

Nominations.

1. (Publication of notice of election.)

2. The day of election shall be fixed by the returning officer as follows: that is to say, in the case of an election for a county or a district borough, not later than the ninth day after the day on which he receives the writ, with an interval of not less than

three clear days between the day on which he gives the notice and the day of election; and in the case of an election for any borough other than a district borough, not later than the fourth day after the day on which he receives the writ, with an interval of not less than two clear days between the day on which he gives the notice and the day of election.

3. (Place of holding the election.)

4. The time appointed for the election shall be such two hours between the hours of 10 in the forenoon and 3 in the afternoon as may be appointed (*h*) by the returning officer, and the returning officer shall attend during those two hours and for one hour after. *(h) See § 14, infra; D, § 1 (3), infra.*

5. Each candidate shall be nominated by a separate nomination-paper, but the same electors or any of them may subscribe as many nomination-papers as there are vacancies to be filled, but no more.

6. Each candidate shall be described in the nomination paper in such manner as in the opinion of the returning officer is calculated to sufficiently identify such candidate; the description shall include his names, his abode, and his rank, profession, or calling, and his surname shall come first in the list of his names. No objection to a nomination paper on the ground of the description of the candidate therein being insufficient, or not being in compliance with this rule, shall be allowed or deemed valid, unless such objection is made by the returning officer or by some other person at or immediately after the time of the delivery of the nomination paper.

7. The returning officer shall supply a form of nomination paper to any registered elector requiring the same during such two hours as the returning officer may fix, between the hours of 10 in the morning and 2 in the afternoon on each day intervening between the day on which notice of the election was given and the day of election, and during the time appointed for the election; but nothing in this Act shall render obligatory the use of a nomination paper supplied by the returning officer, so, however, that the paper be in the form prescribed by this Act.

8. The nomination papers shall be delivered to the returning officer (*i*) at the place of election during the time appointed for the election; and the candidate nominated by each nomina- *(i) Mass., § 6; S. Austr., § 48;*

Queens., § 49;
Belg., § 106;
Ky., § 2;
N. Y., § 4;
Gt. Br., D., § 1
(3), *infra*.

tion paper, and his proposer and seconder, and one other person selected by the candidate, and no person other than aforesaid shall, except for the purpose of assisting the returning officer, be entitled to attend the proceedings during the time appointed for the election.

9. If the election is contested, the returning officer shall, as soon as practicable after adjourning the election, give public notice (*j*) of the day on which the poll will be taken, and of the candidates described as in their respective nomination papers, and of the names of the persons who subscribe the nomination paper of each candidate, and of the order in which the names of the candidates will be printed in the ballot paper, and, in the case of an election for a county, deliver to the postmaster of the principal post-office of the town in which is situate the place of election a paper, signed by himself, containing the names of the candidates nominated, and stating the day on which the poll is to be taken; and the postmaster shall forward the information contained in such paper by telegraph, free of charge, to the several postal telegraph offices situate in the county for which the election is to be held; and such information shall be published forthwith at each such office in the manner in which post-office notices are usually published.

(*j*)
Mass., §§ 14, 15;
S. Austr., § 50;
Queens., §§ 50, 53;
Belg., § 112;
Ky., § 5;
N. Y., § 10;
Gt. Br., D, § 1
(3), *infra*.

10. If any candidate nominated during the time appointed for the election is withdrawn in pursuance of this act, the returning officer shall give public notice of the name of such candidate, and the names of the persons who subscribed the nomination paper of such candidate, as well as of the candidates who stood nominated or were elected.

11. The returning officer shall, on the nomination paper being delivered to him, forthwith publish notice of the name of the person nominated as a candidate, and of the names of his proposer and seconder, by placarding or causing to be placarded the names of the candidate and his proposer and seconder in a conspicuous position outside the building in which the room is situate appointed for the election.

12. A person shall not be entitled to have his name inserted in any ballot paper as a candidate unless he has been nominated in manner provided by this Act; and every person whose nomination paper has been delivered to the returning officer during the time appointed for the election shall be deemed to have been

nominated in manner provided by this Act, unless objection be made to his nomination paper by the returning officer or some other person before the expiration of the time appointed for the election or within one hour afterwards.

13. The returning officer shall decide on the validity of every objection made to a nomination paper (*k*) ; and his decision, if disallowing the objection, shall be final ; but if allowing, the same shall be subject to reversal on petition questioning the election or returns.

(*k*)
Mass., § 7;
Gt. Br., D, § 1
(3), *infra* ; and
NOTE 13, p. 65.

The Poll.

14. The poll shall take place on such day as the returning officer may appoint, not being in the case of an election for a county or a district borough less than two nor more than six clear days, and not being in the case of an election for a borough other than a district borough more than three clear days, after the day fixed for the election (*l*).

(15) At every polling-place the returning officer shall provide a sufficient number of polling-stations for the accommodation of the electors entitled to vote at such polling-place, and shall distribute the polling-stations amongst those electors in such manner as he thinks most convenient; provided that in a district borough there shall be at least one polling-station at each contributory place of such borough.

(*l*)
Mass., § 6;
S. Austr., § 46;
Queens., §§ 48, 49;
Belg., § 105;
Ky., § 2;
N. Y., § 8;
Gt. Br., B, § 4,
ante; D, § 1 (3), *infra*.

16. Each polling-station shall be furnished (*m*) with such number of compartments, in which the voters can mark their votes screened from observation, as the returning officer thinks necessary, so that at least one compartment be provided for every one hundred and fifty electors (*n*) entitled to vote at such polling-station.

(*m*)
Mass., § 21;
S. Austr., § 54;
Queens., § 59;
Belg., § 117;
Ky., § 8;
N. Y., § 20;
and NOTE 5, p. 58.

17. A separate room or separate booth may contain a separate polling-station, or several polling-stations may be constructed in the same room or booth.

(*n*)
Mass., § 21;
Queens., § 59;
Belg., § 118;
Ky., § 8;
N. Y., § 20.

18. No person shall be admitted to vote at any polling-station except the one allotted to him.

19. The returning officer shall give public notice of the situation of polling-stations, and the description of voters entitled to vote at each station, and of the mode in which electors are to vote.

20. The returning officer shall provide each polling-station

with materials for voters to mark the ballot papers, with instruments for stamping thereon the official mark, and with copies of the register of voters or such part thereof as contains the names of the voters allotted to vote at such station. He shall keep the official mark secret; and an interval of not less than seven years shall intervene between the use of the same official mark at elections for the same county or borough.

21. The returning officer shall appoint a presiding officer to preside at each station; and the officer so appointed shall keep order at his station, shall regulate the number of electors to be admitted at a time, and shall exclude all other persons (*o*), except the clerks, the agents of the candidates, and the constables on duty.

(*o*)
Mass., § 21;
S. Austr., § 59;
Queens., § 59;
Belg., § 97;
Ky., § 17;
N. Y., § 20;
and NOTE 1,
p. 52.

22. Every ballot paper shall contain a list of the candidates described as in their respective nomination papers, and arranged (*p*) alphabetically in the order of their surnames, and (if there are two or more candidates with the same surname) of their other names; it shall be in the form set forth in the second schedule to this Act, or as near thereto as circumstances admit, and shall be capable of being folded up.

(*p*)
Mass., § 10;
S. Austr., § 55;
Queens., § 58;
Belg., §§ 114, 115;
Ky., § 4;
N. Y., § 14;
Gt. Br., D, § 1
(6) *infra*;
and NOTE 4,
p. 55.

23. (Provisions relating to the ballot-box.)

24. Immediately before a ballot paper is delivered to an elector, it shall be marked on both sides with the official mark (*q*), either stamped or perforated, and the number, name, and description of the elector as stated in the copy of the register shall be called out, and the number of such elector shall be marked on the counterfoil (*q*), and a mark shall be placed in the register against the number of the elector, to denote that he has received a ballot paper, but without showing the particular ballot paper which he has received.

(*q*)
See Gt. Br., A, § 2, *ante*, and note (c).

25. The elector on receiving the ballot paper shall forthwith proceed into one of the compartments in the polling-station, and there mark (*r*) his paper, and fold it up so as to conceal his vote, and shall then put his ballot-paper, so folded up, into the ballot-box; he shall vote without undue delay, and shall quit the polling-station as soon as he has put his ballot-paper into the ballot-box.

(*r*)
See Gt. Br., A, § 2, *ante*, note (d); and C, "Form of Directions for Voters," *infra*.

26. The presiding officer, on the application of any voter (*s*) who is incapacitated by blindness or other physical cause from voting in the manner prescribed by this Act, or (if the poll be

(*s*)
Mass., § 25;
S. Austr., § 58, VII;

taken on Saturday) of any voter who declares that he is of the Jewish persuasion, and objects on religious grounds to vote in manner prescribed by this Act, or of any voter who makes such a declaration as hereinafter mentioned that he is unable to read, shall, in the presence of the agents of the candidates, cause the vote of such voter to be marked on a ballot paper in manner directed by such voter, and the ballot paper to be placed in the ballot-box, and the name and number on the register of voters of every voter whose vote is marked in pursuance of this rule, and the reason why it is so marked, shall be entered on a list, in this Act called "the list of votes marked by the presiding officer." Queens., § 73; Belg., § 123; Ky., § 10; N. Y., § 25; and NOTE 8, p. 61.

The said declaration, in this Act referred to as "the declaration of inability to read," shall be made by the voter at the time of polling, before the presiding officer, who shall attest it in the form hereinafter mentioned, and no fee, stamp, or other payment shall be charged in respect of such declaration, and the said declaration shall be given to the presiding officer at the time of voting.

27. If a person, representing himself to be a particular elector named on the register, applies for a ballot paper after another person has voted as such elector, the applicant shall, upon duly answering the questions, and taking the oath permitted by law to be asked of and to be administered to voters at the time of polling, be entitled to mark a ballot paper in the same manner as any other voter, but the ballot paper (in this Act called a tendered ballot paper) shall be of a color differing from the other ballot papers, and, instead of being put into the ballot-box, shall be given to the presiding officer, and endorsed by him with the name of the voter and his number in the register of voters, and set aside in a separate packet, and shall not be counted by the returning officer. And the name of the voter and his number on the register shall be entered on a list, in this Act called "the tendered votes list."

28. A voter who has inadvertently dealt with his ballot paper in such manner that it cannot be conveniently used as a ballot paper (*t*) may, on delivering to the presiding officer the ballot paper so inadvertently dealt with, and proving the fact of the inadvertence to the satisfaction of the presiding officer, obtain another ballot paper in the place of the ballot paper so delivered (*t*) Mass., § 24; S. Austr., § 58, VIII; Belg., § 125; Ky., § 9; N. Y., § 24.

up (in this Act called a spoilt ballot paper), and the spoilt ballot paper shall be immediately cancelled.

29. The presiding officer of each station, as soon as practicable after the close of the poll, shall, in the presence of the agents of the candidates, make up into separate packets sealed with his own seal and the seals of such agents of the candidates as desire to affix their seals, —

(1.) Each ballot-box in use at his station, unopened, but with the key attached; and

(2.) The unused and spoilt ballot papers placed together; and

(3.) The tendered ballot papers; and

(4.) The marked copies of the register of voters, and the counterfoils of the ballot papers; and

(5.) The tendered votes list, and the list of votes marked by the presiding officer, and a statement of the number of the voters whose votes are so marked by the presiding officer under the heads "physical incapacity," "Jews," and "unable to read," and the declarations of inability to read; and shall deliver such packets to the returning officer.

30. The packets shall be accompanied by a statement made by such presiding officer, showing the number of ballot papers entrusted to him, and accounting for them under the heads of ballot-papers in the ballot-box, unused, spoilt, and tendered ballot papers, which statement is in this Act referred to as the ballot paper account.

Counting Votes.

31-34. (Provisions for conducting the counting of the votes.)

34. Before the returning officer proceeds to count the votes, he shall, in the presence of the agents of the candidates, open each ballot-box, and taking out the papers therein, shall count and record the number thereof, and then mix together the whole of the ballot papers contained in the ballot-boxes. The returning officer, while counting and recording the number of ballot papers and counting the votes, shall keep the ballot-papers with their faces upwards, and take all proper precautions for preventing any person from seeing the numbers printed on the backs of such ballot papers.

35. (Provision as to the time during which the counting shall take place.)

GREAT BRITAIN AND IRELAND. 97

36. . . . The returning officer shall report to the Clerk of the Crown in Chancery the number of ballot papers rejected and not counted by him under the several heads of—
1. Want of official mark;
2. Voting for more candidates than entitled to;
3. Writing or mark by which voter may be identified;
4. Unmarked, or void for uncertainty;

and shall, on request, allow any agents of the candidates, before such report is sent, to copy it.

37–39. (Provisions for sealing all packets, etc., and forwarding them to the Clerk of the Crown in Chancery.)

40. (Inspection of rejected ballot-papers to be allowed only upon order of the proper tribunal.)

41. No person shall, except by order of the House of Commons or any tribunal having cognizance of petitions complaining of undue returns or undue elections, open the sealed packet of counterfoils after the same has been once sealed up, or be allowed to inspect any counted ballot papers in the custody of the Clerk of the Crown in Chancery; such order may be made subject to such conditions as to persons, time, place, and mode of opening as the House or tribunal making the order may think expedient; provided that on making and carrying into effect any such order, care shall be taken that the mode in which any particular elector has voted shall not be discovered until he has been proved to have voted, and his vote has been declared by a competent court to be invalid.

42–43. (Further provision as to the inspection of ballot-papers, etc.)

General Provisions (44–63).

46. Where the returning officer is required or authorized by this Act to give any public notice, he shall carry such requirement into effect by advertisements, placards, handbills, or such other means as he thinks best calculated to afford information to the electors.

50. The presiding officer may do, by the clerks appointed to assist him (*u*) any act which he is required or authorized to do by this Act at a polling-station, except ordering the arrest, exclusion, or ejection from the polling-station of any person.

54. Every returning officer, and every officer, clerk, or agent

(*u*) Mass., § 22; S. Austr., § 58, IV.; Queens., § 71; Belg., § 123;

Ky., § 7;
N. Y., § 21;
and Note 6,
p. 59.

authorized to attend at a polling-station, or at the counting of the votes, shall, before the opening of the poll, make a statutory declaration of secrecy, in the presence, if he is the returning officer, of a justice of the peace, and if he is any other officer or agent, of a justice of the peace or of the returning officer. . . .

56. In reckoning time for the purposes of this Act, Sunday, Christmas Day, Good Friday, and any day set apart for a public fast or public thanksgiving, shall be excluded (*v*) ; and where anything is required by this Act to be done on any day which falls on the above-mentioned days, such thing may be done on the next day, unless it is one of the days excluded as above-mentioned.

(*v*)
S. Austr., § 101;
Ky., § 2;
and Note 14,
p. 65.

PART II. (Application of the foregoing Rules to Municipal Elections).

C.

SECOND SCHEDULE.

1. *Form of Nomination Paper in Parliamentary Election.*

We, the undersigned, A. B. of   in the   of   , and C. D. of   in the   of   , being electors for the   of   , do hereby nominate the following person as a proper person to serve as member for the said   in Parliament:

Surname.	Other Names.	Abode.	Rank, Profession, or Occupation.
Brown	John	52, George St., Bristol	Merchant
Jones	William David	High Elms, Wilts	Esquire
Merton	Hon. George Travis, commonly called Viscount	Swanworth, Berks	Viscount
Smith	Henry Sydney	72, High St., Bath	Attorney

(Signed) A. B.
C. D.

We, the undersigned, being registered electors of   , do hereby assent to the nomination of the above-mentioned *John Brown* as a proper person to serve as a member for the said   in Parliament.

(Signed) E. F. of
G. H. of
I. J. of
K. L. of
M. N. of
O. P. of
Q. R. of
S. T. of

2. *Form of Ballot-Paper.*

Form of Front of Ballot Paper.

Counterfoil No.			
	1	BROWN. (John Brown, of 52, George St., Bristol, Merchant).	
	2	JONES. (William David Jones, of High Elms, Wilts, Esq.)	
NOTE: *The counterfoil is to have a number to correspond with that on the back of the Ballot-Paper.*	3	MERTON. (Hon. George Travis, commonly called Viscount, of Swanworth, Berks).	
	4	SMITH. (Henry Sydney Smith, of 72, High St., Bath, Attorney).	

Form of Back of Ballot Paper.

No.
18 . Election for county [or borough, or ward].

Form of Directions for the Guidance of the Voter in voting, which shall be printed in conspicuous Characters, and placarded outside every Polling-Station and in every Compartment of every Polling-Station.

The voter may vote for candidate .

The voter will go into one of the compartments, and, with the pencil provided in the compartment, place a cross (*w*) on the right hand side, opposite the name of each candidate for whom he votes, thus **X**.

(*w*) See Gt. Br., A, § 2, *ante*, note (*d*), and B, § 25.

GREAT BRITAIN AND IRELAND. 101

The voter will then fold up the ballot paper so as to show the official mark on the back, and leaving the compartment, will, without showing the front of the paper to any person, show the official mark on the back to the presiding officer, and then, in the presence of the presiding officer, put the paper into the ballot-box, and forthwith quit the polling-station.

If the voter inadvertently spoils a ballot-paper, he can return it to the officer, who will, if satisfied of the inadvertence, give him another paper.

If the voter votes for more than candidate , or places any mark on the paper by which he may be afterwards identified, his ballot paper will be void and will not be counted.

If the voter takes a ballot paper out of the polling-station, or deposits in the box any other paper than the one given him by the officer, he will be guilty of a misdemeanor, and be subject to imprisonment for any term not exceeding six months, with or without hard labor.

Note. These directions shall be illustrated by examples of the ballot paper.

D.

The regulations governing the conduct of municipal elections were partially altered by the Municipal Elections Act, 1875 (38–9 Vict. c. 40), the sections embodying material changes being herewith given.

Municipal Elections Act, 1875.

1. . . . (3) Every nomination paper subscribed as aforesaid shall be delivered by the candidate himself, or his proposer or seconder, to the town clerk (x), seven days at least before the day of election (y), and before 5 o'clock in the afternoon of the last day on which any such nomination paper may by law be delivered; the town clerk shall forthwith send notice of such nomination to each person nominated. The mayor shall attend at the town hall on the day next after the last day for the delivery of nomina-

(x) See B, § 8, *ante*, note (*i*).
(y) See B, § 14, *ante*, note (*h*).

tions to the town clerk between the hours of 2 and 4 in the afternoon, and shall decide on the validity of every objection made to a nomination paper (*z*), such objection to be made in writing. . . . The decision of the mayor, which shall be given in writing, shall, if disallowing any objection to a nomination paper, be final, but if allowing the same shall be subject to reversal on petition questioning the election or return. . . . The town clerk shall (*a*) at least four days before the day of election cause the surnames and other names of all persons duly nominated, with their respective places of abode and descriptions, and the names of the persons subscribing their respective nomination papers, as proposers and seconders, to be printed and placed on the door of the town hall, and in some conspicuous parts of the borough or ward for which such election is to be held.

. . . 7. When more candidates are nominated at any municipal election than there are vacancies to be filled at such election, any of such candidates may withdraw (*b*) from his candidature by notice signed by him and delivered to the town clerk not later than two o'clock in the afternoon of the day next after the last day for the delivery of nomination papers to the town clerk. . . .

. . . 6. At the poll at any election of auditors and assessors one ballot paper only shall be used by any person voting. In such ballot paper (*c*) the names of the candidates for the respective offices shall be separate and distinguished, so as to show the office for which they are respectively candidates; and the ballot paper shall be in the form No. 3, set forth in the first schedule to this Act, or to the like effect. . . .

The provisions of this Act have been embodied in the Municipal Corporations Act, 1882 (45–6 Vict. c. 50), and are now in force by virtue of the latter Act. The provisions corresponding to those quoted above are contained for the most part in Schedule III., Part II., of the Act of 1882.

Margin notes:
(z) See B, § 13, ante, note (k).
(a) See B, § 9, ante, note (j).
(b) See A, § 1, ante, note (b).
(c) See B, § 22, ante, note (p).

3. *Form of Ballot Paper for Municipal Elections.*

Form of Front of Ballot Paper.

FOR AUDITORS.

Counterfoil No.			
	1	CADE. (John Cade, of 22, Wellclose Place, Accountant.)	
	2	JOHNSON. (Charles Johnson, of 7, Albion St., Gentleman.)	
	3	THOMPSON. (William Thompson, of 14, Queen St., Silversmith.)	

NOTE: *The counterfoil is to have a number to correspond with that on the back of the Ballot-Paper.*

FOR REVISING ASSESSORS.

1	BACON. (Charles Bacon, of 29, New St., Solicitor.)	
2	BYRON. (James Byron, of 45, George St., Commission Agent.)	
3	WILSON. (George Wilson, of 22, Hanover Square, Gentleman.)	

E.

By the Parliamentary Elections (Returning Officers) Act, 1875 (38–9 Vict. c. 84), the expenses of parliamentary elections are placed upon the candidates in equal shares, or upon the nominators of a candidate, if he was nominated without his consent. To this extent the provisions of the Ballot Act are altered so that if the returning officer exercises his right (§ 3 of the above Act) to require

(d) Queens., §§ 49, 55; Ky., § 2; and NOTE 15, p. 65.

security (d) from the candidates, and a candidate fails to offer that security (the proper sum being estimated according to a fixed schedule) within one hour from the time when nominations are closed, his nomination is a nullity. The above Act was amended by the Parliamentary Elections (Returning Officers) Act, 1885, but only in respect to the amount of security to be required.

V. BELGIUM.

A. *Electoral Codes*, 1872, *as amended by Consolidated Election Laws*, 1878.
B. *Law of* 21 *May*, 1884.

A.

ELECTORAL CODE, 1872, AS AMENDED BY CONSOLIDATED ELECTION LAWS, 1878.

[TITLE I. QUALIFICATIONS OF VOTERS.]

[TITLE II. REGISTRATION.]

[TITLE III. ELECTION DISTRICTS.]

TITLE IV. CONDUCT OF ELECTIONS (Arts. 96–166).

Chap. I. *General Regulations for the preservation of Order, etc.*

Art. 97. The presiding election officer of the district or of the polling-station shall have sole authority to enforce order in the premises where the election is held; he may delegate this authority to one of the officers at the polling-place for the purpose of maintaining order in the waiting-room while the voters are being called in.

Only candidates and voters of the district shall be admitted to the premises where the election takes place. But during the voting and the counting of votes they shall not remain (*a*) in that part of the premises where these proceedings take place.

(*a*) Mass., § 21; S. Austr., § 59; Queens., § 59; Gt. Br., B, § 21; Ky., § 17; N. Y., § 20; and NOTE 1, p. 52.

Chap. II. (applying only to national and provincial elections).

Section I. *Candidates.*

Art. 105. Candidates must be proposed at least six clear days before the day of election (*b*).

(*b*)
Mass., § 6;
S. Austr., § 46;
Queens., §§ 48, 49;
Gt. Br., B, §§ 4, 14, D, § 1 (3);
Ky., § 2;
N. Y., § 8.

Art. 106. The nomination paper must be signed (1) in an election for the legislature, by at least fifty electors (*c*) in the arrondissements, which, when an entire legislature is to be elected, are entitled to more than four members, and by thirty electors in other arrondissements; (2) in a provincial election, by at least twenty-five electors (*c*) in the cantons which are entitled to four or more councillors, and by ten electors in other cantons.

(*c*)
Mass., § 4;
S. Austr., § 48;
Queens., § 49;
Gt. Br., A, § 1;
Ky., § 2;
N. Y., § 5;
Belg., § 155,
infra; and
NOTE 2, p. 53.

Nomination papers shall be delivered by three of the signers thereof to the presiding officer of the chief polling-place (*d*), who shall give a receipt therefor. They shall indicate the surname, first name, residence, and occupation of the candidates and of the electors who present them, and shall be dated and signed. The candidates shall be entered on the ballot in alphabetical order, and when members of the senate and of the chamber of representatives are to be elected at the same time, their names shall be arranged in separate groups.

(*d*)
Mass., § 6;
S. Austr., § 48;
Queens., § 49;
Gt. Br., B, § 8, D, § 1(3);
Ky., § 2;
N. Y., § 4.

Art. 107. A person proposed as a candidate shall accept (*e*) in writing, signed by himself, and delivered to the presiding officer of the chief polling-place. When candidates present themselves together and form an entire group [equal in number to the number of members to be elected], the acceptance shall so state. Candidates for the legislature may indicate the party appellation which they wish printed at the head of their group.

(*e*)
S. Austr., § 48;
NOTE 3, p. 54.

An acceptance may be made at the same time with the nomination.

Art. 108. Candidates shall, at the time of accepting, designate, as agents to be present at the polls, as many electors as there are polling-places, and an equal number of substitutes. A candidate himself may be designated as agent or as substitute.

BELGIUM. 107

Art. 109. The requirements of Arts. 107 and 108 shall be fulfilled five clear days before the day of election.

Arts. 110–111. (Provision, in further detail, for the appointment of agents for the polling-places.)

Art. 112. At the expiration of the period within which nominations may be made, the election officers of the chief polling-place shall make up the list of candidates for whom votes may validly be given on the day of election. This list shall be immediately posted (*f*) in all the towns of the arrondissement or the canton. The posted list shall contain in large letters, in black ink, the names of the candidates in the form of the ballot as hereafter described, and shall in addition indicate the first name, occupation, and residence of each candidate, and shall also contain the instructions annexed as No. I.

The presiding officer of the chief polling-place, at the request of the candidates or of the electors who presented them, shall communicate (*g*) to them the official list of candidates not later than the fourth day before the day of election.

(*f*) Mass., §§ 14, 15; S. Austr., § 50; Queens., §§ 50, 53; Gt. Br., B, § 9, D, § 1(3); Ky., § 5; N. Y., § 10.

(*g*) See (*f*) *supra.*

Section II. *Ballots.*

Art. 113. At the expiration of the time allowed for presenting candidates, the election officers of the chief polling-place shall prepare the ballots and cause them to be printed on official paper.

Art. 114. Candidates to the legislature who present themselves together and form an entire group shall be placed in a single column, arranged in alphabetical order for each Chamber, the candidates for the Senate coming first (*h*). The party appellation, as indicated according to Art. 107, shall be printed at the head of the column. When there are more members than one to be elected, candidates presented independently shall be placed in alphabetical order in a special column. Each column shall be printed in ink of a different color; the whole ballot being prepared according to the annexed model No. II.

(*h*) Mass., § 10; S. Austr., § 55; Queens., § 58; Gt. Br., B, § 22; D, §1 (6); Ky., § 4; N. Y., § 14; and NOTE 4, p. 55.

Art. 115. Candidates for the provincial councils who

present themselves together and form an entire group shall be placed in a single column in alphabetical order (*i*). The first column shall contain the group in which occurs the name first in alphabetical order, and so on for the other groups, whether entire or partial.

The election officers of the chief polling-place shall cause the ballots to be printed or written in black ink. Those who present themselves together and form an entire group may request that a distinctive device be placed at the head of their group; the whole being prepared according to the annexed model No. III.

Art. 116. The use of all other ballots is forbidden.

Section III. *Of Polling Arrangements and the Process of Voting.*

Art. 117. The polling place and the separate compartments in which the electors must record or determine upon their votes shall be constructed (*j*) according to the annexed model No. IV. But the dimensions and arrangement thereof may be modified according to the requirements of the premises or the needs of the occasion.

Art. 118. There shall be at least one compartment or separate shelf for every 100 electors (*k*).

Art. 119. Instructions, as contained in the annexed model No. I., shall be placarded on the outside of each polling-place, in the waiting-room, and within each separate compartment.

Art. 120. The electors shall be called in alphabetical order from a list containing the name, first name, age, occupation, and residence of every elector in the district or polling-place. Any charges of error in this list shall be decided upon by the election officers, having regard only to the official lists arranged by towns and posted according to Art. 102.

Art. 121. (Provides that no one shall vote whose name is not on the list or who cannot present a certificate of qualification from the proper authorities.)

Art. 122. As one elector leaves the voting-place, the

clerk shall call another so that the electors shall succeed each other in the compartments without cessation.

Art. 123. The elector when called shall approach and receive from the hands of the presiding officer (*l*) a ballot folded at right angles into four parts, and stamped (*m*) on the back with a stamp indicating the number of the polling-place, and the date of the election. He shall proceed directly to one of the compartments, shall there mark his vote, shall return and show to the presiding officer the ballot folded properly into four parts, the stamp on the outside, shall drop it into the ballot-urn, and shall leave the voting-room.

When it is made to appear that a voter is blind or infirm (*n*), the presiding officer shall permit him to have a guide or assistant accompany him into the compartment. The names of both shall be preserved in the official report of the proceedings.

Art. 124. If the elector wishes to give his vote to all the candidates of a single group, he shall mark (*o*) with a pencil a cross in the square reserved for the purpose at the head of the group of candidates. If he wishes to give his vote to certain candidates upon the same or different lists, he shall mark (*o*) with a pencil a cross in the square reserved for this purpose opposite the name of each of the candidates for whom he votes. When there is but one member to elect, the vote shall be expressed as in the former case above, no square being printed opposite the candidate's name.

Every cross, although imperfectly made, shall be a valid expression of the vote (*p*), unless an intention is manifest to render the ballot recognizable.

Art. 125. If the elector inadvertently mars (*q*) the ballot which has been delivered to him, he may request another from the presiding officer, upon giving up to him the first, which shall be immediately cancelled.

Art. 126. The clerk shall check on the list the name of each elector who answers at the time of the first or the second call. When an elector receives a ballot from the

(*l*) Mass., § 22; S. Austr., § 58, IV.; Queens., § 71; Gt. Br., B, § 50; Ky., § 7; N. Y., § 21; and NOTE 6, p. 59.

(*m*) Mass., § 10; S. Austr., § 57; Queens., § 71; Gt. Br., A, § 2; B, § 24; Ky., §§ 4, 7; N. Y., § 21; Belg., § 151, *infra*; and NOTE 7, p. 59.

(*n*) Mass., § 25; S. Austr., § 58, VII.; Queens., § 73; Gt. Br., B, § 26; Ky., § 10; N. Y., § 25; and NOTE 8, p. 61.

(*o*) Mass, § 23; S. Austr., § 58, VI.; Queens., § 73; Gt. Br., A, § 2, B, § 25; C, "Form of Directions for voters;" Ky., § 9; N. Y., § 22; Belg., B, § 1, *infra*; and NOTE 9, p. 62.

(*p*) See (*r*), *infra*, p. 110.

(*q*) Mass., § 24; S. Austr., § 58, VIII.; Gt. Br., B, § 23; Ky., § 9; N. Y., § 24.

hands of the presiding officer, one of the inspectors shall enter his name on a special list of voters.

Art. 127. There shall be a second call for those electors who were not present when first called. When the second call is over, the presiding officer or his deputy shall ask the assemblage if there are any electors present who have not voted. Those who present themselves immediately shall be allowed to vote. When this has been done, the poll shall be declared closed.

Art. 128. The elector may not remain in the compartment longer than is necessary to prepare his ballot.

Art. 129. When the poll is closed, the election officers shall place in separate sealed envelopes the ballots returned according to Art. 125, and the unused ballots. The number of returned ballots shall be recorded in the official report, and the envelope containing them shall be annexed thereto. The unused ballots shall be returned by the election officers of the chief polling-place to the superintendent of registration of the province.

Art. 130. No one shall be compelled to disclose the manner in which he voted, whether at a preliminary examination, a trial, or a parliamentary inquiry.

Section IV. *Counting the Votes.*

(*r*)
Mass., § 26;
S. Austr., § 64;
Queens., § 76;
Gt. Br., § 2;
Ky., § 11;
N.Y., §§ 13. 28;
Belg., § 124,
ante; and
Note 10, p. 63.

Art. 147. The following ballots shall be void (*r*) :

1. All ballots other than those whose use is permitted by this act :

2. All ballots expressing no choice, or giving more than one vote to the same person, or containing more votes than there are members to be elected to either of the legislative chambers or to the provincial councils :

3. All ballots which by a sign, erasure, or other mark of any sort, not authorized by law, are rendered recognizable, and all ballots altered in form or dimensions, or containing within them a paper or other thing.

(*s*)
See (m), *ante.*

Art. 151. The State shall furnish the election paper, which shall be stamped before being delivered (*s*) to the presiding officer of the chief polling-place.

The government shall fix the dimensions of ballots according to the number of members to be elected. Ballots for the same district at the same election shall be of the same dimensions.[1]

Art. 152. It shall be the duty of the capital town of each arrondissement to take charge of, renew, and repair the partitions, shelves, and other material furnished to them by the State. The partitions, railings, shelves, stamping-instruments, and stamps shall be furnished by the provinces to the other towns which are capitals of cantons; and it shall be the duty of these towns to take charge of, renew, and repair these materials.

Art. 153. All other expenses incident to elections (except the electoral registers in several towns, which are charged upon the province) shall be borne by the town in which the election takes place.

Chap. III. (Application of the foregoing principles to Elections in Towns.)

Art. 155. (As amended by the law of 26 Aug. 1878) (*t*). Nominations of candidates shall be signed (*u*) in towns of

(*t*) *Supplement*, etc., p. 39.

(*u*) See (c), *ante*.

More than 10,000 inhabitants, by at least 20 electors;
From 5,000 to 10,000 inhabitants, by at least 10 electors;
From 3,000 to 5,000 inhabitants, by at least 5 electors;

and in towns of less than 3,000 inhabitants, by 3 electors, among whom may be the candidates themselves.

TITLE V: PENALTIES (Arts. 167-191).

Art. 168. The counterfeiting of official ballots shall be punished as a falsification of a public writing.

Art. 169. Any person who shall append the signature of another or of a fictitious person to a nomination-paper,

---

[1] By the laws of 18 Jan. and 17 Sept., 1878 (*Supplement*, etc., pp. 19, 25), the size of the ballots is fixed as follows, the first figure representing the width: In districts having less than 6 members, 21 × 21 cm.; having from 6 to 12 members, 24 × 24 cm.; having more than 12 members, 21 × 34 cm.; and in towns (general elections) 21 × 34 cm.

to an acceptance of a nomination, or to an appointment of agents shall be deemed guilty of falsifying a private writing.

Art. 183. Every presiding officer, inspector, or clerk of a polling-place, and every agent of a candidate, who shall disclose the contents of one or more ballots shall be fined not less than 500 f., and not more than 8000 f., and in addition may be deprived, for a period not exceeding ten years, of the right to act as election officer or agent, or to vote or to be voted for.

[TITLE VI: QUALIFICATIONS FOR HOLDING OFFICE.]

[TITLE VII: CONSTITUTION OF THE LEGISLATIVE CHAMBERS, PROVINCIAL AND TOWN COUNCILS.]

[TITLE VIII: REPEALS AND MISCELLANEOUS PROVISIONS.]

B.

Law of 21 *May,* 1884, *repealing art.* 124, *ante.*

ART. 1. If the elector wishes to give his vote to all the candidates of a single group, he shall (*v*) blacken with the instrument ("*estampille*") placed at his disposition the white point in the centre of the square placed at the head of the list of candidates.

If the elector wishes to give his vote to certain candidates upon the same or different lists, he shall (*v*) blacken as before the white point in the centre of the square placed opposite the name of each candidate for whom he votes. . . . Every impression made in the square with the instrument and covering the white point, even though incomplete, confused, or otherwise defective, shall be a valid expression of the vote, unless an intention is manifest to render the ballot recognizable.

(*v*) See (*o*), *ante.*

BELGIUM.

MODEL No. II.

Legislative Ballot (actual size about 10 in. square).

ANVERS.   (National Seal.)   ELECTION DU........

[Blue.]	[Black.]	[Carmine.]
For Senator (Liberal).	For Senator [all others].	For Senator (Catholic).
1 DESMET	1 AMMAN	1 MABILLE
2 EVERAERT	2 DELVAL	2 PEPIN
3 NELSON	3	3 VANSTUPPEN
For Representative (Liberal).	For Representative [all others].	For Representative (Catholic).
1 DUBOIS	1 UYTERELST	1 ABELOOT
2 GEIRTS	2 VAN LOY	2 DEBOECK
3 MATERLING		3 HOMMEN
4 NICK		4 HOTTOIS
5 VANDENTOCK		5 LINSACK
6 VARMON		6 VAN DIEZT

MODEL No. III.
Provincial Ballot.

ÉLECTION DU PROVINCE DE............, 18...

	✶		◇		○
1	ABADIE	1	BERTRAND	1	COLIN
2	DELCAMPS	2	CORNET	2	DALTON
3	JACQUES	3	DUCANGE	3	HERMAND
4	NIEMAND	4	MAENHOUT	4	NICOLAS
5	PEETERS	5	ROBIN	5	STEVENS
6	XHOFFER	6	VERTBOIS	6	TILQUIN

MODEL No. IV.

Polling Arrangements.

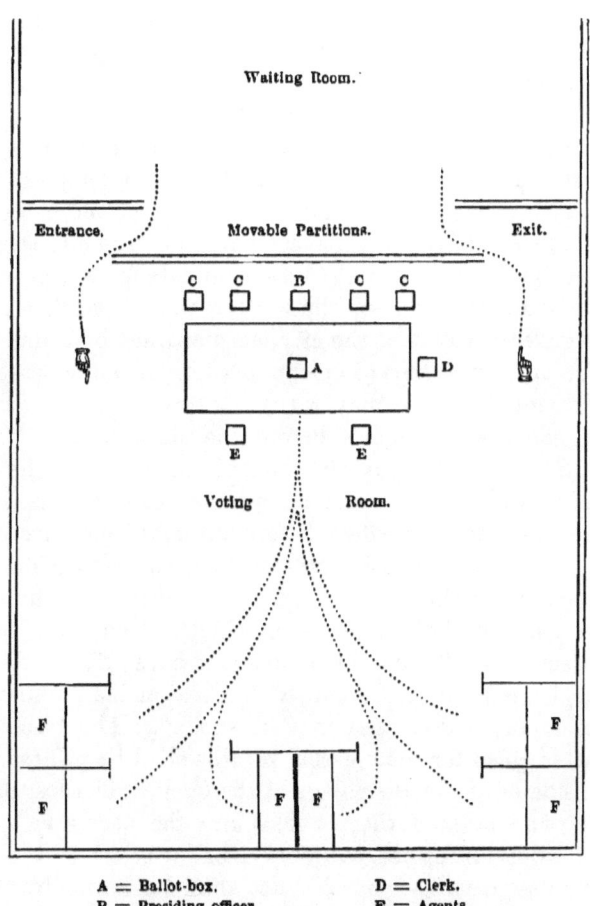

A = Ballot-box.
B = Presiding officer.
C = Inspectors.
D = Clerk.
E = Agents.
F = Compartments.

VI. — KENTUCKY.

AN ACT TO REGULATE MUNICIPAL ELECTIONS IN THE CITY OF LOUISVILLE (Approved Feb. 24, 1888).

SECTION 1. (The provisions of the act are applicable to elections of municipal officers, with certain exceptions, in Louisville.)

<small>(a) Mass., § 4; S. Austr., § 48; Queens., § 49; Gt. Br., A, § 1; Belg., §§ 106, 155; N. Y., § 5; and NOTE 2, p. 53.</small>

<small>(b) Queens., §§ 49, 55; Gt. Br., E.</small>

<small>(c) Mass., § 6; S. Austr., § 48; Queens., § 49; Gt. Br., B, § 8; D, § 1 (3); Belg., § 106; N. Y., § 4.</small>

<small>(d) Mass., § 6; S. Austr., § 46; Queens., §§ 48, 49; Gt. Br., B., §§ 4, 14; D, § 1 (3); Belg., § 105; N. Y., § 8.</small>

<small>(e) S. Austr., § 101; Gt. Br., B, § 56; and NOTE 14, p. 65.</small>

<small>(f) Mass., § 12; S. Austr., § 56; Queens., § 58; N. Y., § 16.</small>

SEC. 2. In order to have their names printed on the ballots hereinafter described, candidates must be nominated as follows: A candidate for one ward must be proposed by the written petition of ten or more registered voters (a) of the ward, accompanied by the city treasurer's receipt for five dollars (b); a candidate for the city at large must be proposed by the written petition of fifty or more registered voters of the city, accompanied by a like receipt for twenty dollars (b); the petition in either case to be presented to the mayor (c) not less than ten days (d), Sundays included (e), before the election.

SEC. 3. It shall be the duty of the mayor of the city to cause to be printed and bound and ready for distribution, not less than three days before any municipal election, one book of stubs and ballots for each voting precinct in said city, and within such three days to distribute these books among the clerks of such precincts. The book for each precinct shall contain as many leaves (f) as there are registered voters therein, with a reasonable number added to supply ballots that may be spoiled. The form hereinafter given for the election returns shall be printed on the inside of one of the covers of the book. The cost of printing and binding these books, and the necessary expenses of all publications, stationery, ballot-boxes and compartments prescribed by this act shall be borne by the city.

Should the mayor be absent from the city, or prevented by sickness from acting, the duties imposed by this section upon him shall be performed by the city attorney.

SEC. 4. Each stub in such books shall have printed on it a consecutive number, commencing with number one, and shall be worded as follows: —

Consecutive number — (After these words the consecutive number shall be printed, beginning with one, and increasing in regular numerical order).

Name of voter — (After these words the clerk shall set down the voter's name).

Registered residence — (After these words the clerk is to set down the voter's residence as found in the registration book of the precinct).

The ballot shall be printed on the same leaf with, and shall be separated from the stub by a perforated line; and it shall be divided by heavy black lines into two columns, and these again by horizontal black lines into divisions for the different offices to be voted for, or questions to be determined. Each division shall be substantially in the following form (g) : —

For Mayor { John Brown, William Smith, James Williams, }

(g) Mass., § 10; S. Austr., § 55; Queens., § 58; Gt. Br., B, § 22; D, § 1 (6); Belg., §§ 114, 115; N. Y., § 14; and NOTE 4, p. 55.

arranging the names in the alphabetical order of their surnames, and if several candidates have the same surname, in the order of their given names; and in like manner for the other city offices to be filled, in this order: Mayor, Receiver of City Taxes, Treasurer, Auditor. Then, if any question be submitted, —

For ——— tax (or other measure) { Yes. No. }

Should there be hereafter other officers to be voted for by the whole city, proper divisions are to be added for them. In the second column similar divisions shall be printed: For Alderman, for Councilman, for School Trustee, with the names of the candidates put after them in the manner above indicated: Provided, that the ballot shall have only one column when only representatives of wards or when only officers for the whole city are to be elected.

The mayor shall cause the contents and form of the ballot, in the exact shape and size in which it is to be used for the city at large and for each ward, to be published (*h*) in one or more of the daily newspapers that do the city printing on the day preceding the election, or in handbill form, in his discretion; in which latter case he shall cause said handbill to be properly circulated and distributed, to the end that the voters may become familiar therewith.

SEC. 6. (Division of the wards into precincts.)

SEC. 7. When a voter has given his name, and the same is found on the registration list, and he is found otherwise qualified, the clerk of the election shall put the voter's name on a stub in the book, together with the voter's registered residence, and the stub-book shall, for this purpose, take the place of a poll-book. The clerk (*i*) shall tear the ballot off the stub and write his own name on the back thereof (*j*), and hand it thus indorsed to the voter. He shall also hand the voter an envelope or paper bag, and shall then check the voter's name off on the registration book.

SEC. 8. (A ballot-box is to be provided by the Mayor.) The Mayor shall also cause to be set up, at each voting place, wooden compartments (*k*), one for every 175 registered voters or fraction thereof (*l*), about six feet in height, and about three feet square; one side to open and shut as a door, with a narrow shelf affixed to the opposite side. The clerk of each precinct shall put into each of these compartments lead pencils hung by strings.

SEC. 9. Each voter, when furnished with a ballot and envelope or paper bag, must step alone into one of the compartments and close the door behind him, and while within the same he shall put (*m*) on his ballot, after each name of the candidate whom he prefers, a pencil mark in the shape of an oblique cross, in substance thus ×, and in like manner after the answer "yes" or "no" to any question, submitted to the people. While still in the compartment he shall fold the ballot and put it in the envelope or paper bag furnished to him. Should he inadvertently spoil a ballot (*n*) he may return it and receive in place thereof one other ballot; the spoiled ballot thus returned shall be preserved by the clerk, and the fact shall be noted by him by writing the word "spoiled" on the stub. (A voter may cast his vote for a person not nominated, as provided in section 2, above, by writing the name of such person after that of the office to which he would have him elected, and making the mark hereinabove provided for after such name) (*o*).

Queens., § 73; Gt. Br., A, § 2, B, § 25, C, "Form of Directions for Voters;" Belg., A, § 124, B, § 1; N. Y., § 22; and Note 9, p. 62.

(*n*) Mass., § 24; S. Austr., § 58, VIII.; Gt. Br, B, § 28; Belg., § 125; N. Y., § 24.

SEC. 10. When a voter is, and avows himself to be, blind (*p*), and is found to be such by the concurrence of both judges and the sheriff of the precinct, the clerk shall accompany him to one of the compartments and mark the ballot at his dictation, and the word "blind" shall be put on the stub under such voter's name.

(*o*) Mass., § 10; N. Y., § 13; and Note 16, p. 66.

(*p*) Mass., § 25; S. Austr., § 58, VII.; Queens., § 73; Gt. Br., B, § 26; Belg., § 123; N. Y., § 25; and Note 8, p. 61.

SEC. 11. A ballot which appears by its paper or type not to have been taken from the stub-book, or which is not indorsed with the clerk's signature, or which contains any marks or writing upon it other than provided for by law, or which is put into an envelope or paper bag having any mark or writing upon it, or two or more ballots put into the same receptacle, shall be void (*q*). When a voter marks more candidates for one office than he has a right to vote for, the ballot shall be void as to that office only.

(*q*) Mass., § 26; S. Austr., § 64; Queens., § 76; Gt. Br., A, § 2; Belg., §§ 124, 147; N. Y., §§ 13, 28; and Note 10, p. 63.

SEC. 12. A voter shall not occupy a compartment for more than three minutes (*r*), and shall, as soon as he leaves it, hand his ballot, folded and within the envelope or paper bag, to the judges, who shall immediately, in the voter's presence, drop it in the ballot-box, affording him full opportunity to see it dropped in for himself; whereupon the voter shall at once withdraw from the room to the distance hereinafter prescribed. The sheriff of the precinct shall enforce the provision limiting the voter's stay in the com-

(*r*) Mass., § 23; N. Y., § 12.

partment, and requiring his immediate withdrawal after voting.

SEC. 13. (Provision for preserving the ballot of one who claims to vote upon a name already voted upon.)

SEC. 14. (Closing the polls and counting the ballots.) The ballots on which questions are raised by one of the judges, or which are rejected, the ballots counted as valid, those marked "voted on before," and the spoiled ballots, shall all be put in separate sealed packages, and the number and description of ballots indorsed upon each package. The officers of each precinct shall return these packages, together with the stub-book, to the Mayor on the night following the election. . . .

SEC. 15. (Form of return for election officers.)

SEC. 16. (Provisions relating to the choice of election officers, and their duties.)

(s) Mass., § 21; S. Austr., § 59; Queens., § 59; Gt. Br., B, § 21; Belg., § 97; N. Y., § 20; and NOTE 1, p. 52.

SEC. 17. The following persons and no other (s) shall be permitted to remain in the room in which the election is held, with the judges, sheriff, and clerk: One agent of each candidate who has been named in writing by the candidate as the only, or as one of two agents for such precinct: Provided such writing has been deposited, before the opening of the polls, with the clerk of the election, who shall set down the name of such agent, and that of the candidate he represents, in the stub-book before the voting begins. These agents have the right to challenge persons offering to vote, but are not allowed to persuade, influence, or intimidate any one in the choice of his candidate, or to attempt doing so, nor shall they go forward and backward between the polls and those awaiting their turn.

SEC. 18. The voting-places at all elections under this act shall be so arranged as to leave a clear space of fifty feet between the room or inclosure in which the voting is done and those waiting their turn to vote, or other persons present at such election; and the sheriff of election and the police stationed at said precinct shall keep all persons, except the officers of the election, those voting at the time, and the candidates or agents of candidates hereinabove mentioned, at that distance from the room or inclosure.

SEC. 19. Any policeman who fails to keep all persons at the lawful distance from the room or inclosure as hereinabove provided . . . shall thereby vacate his office as policeman, and it shall be the duty of the Mayor to dismiss him at once from the force.

SEC. 20. . . . *Subsect.* 6. Any officer of election who gives any information as to any one's vote, which he has obtained in the course of or by color of his office, except when compelled to do so in the course of a judicial investigation, shall be guilty of a misdemeanor, and shall, on conviction, pay a fine of not less than fifty nor more than one hundred dollars for each offence.

. . . *Subsect.* 8. Any judge or sheriff of an election who corruptly and falsely declares a voter to be blind, under section ten of this act, shall be liable to the penalties imposed upon officers of election by subsection 6 of this section for the acts therein denounced.

. . . *Subsect.* 10. Any judge, sheriff, or clerk of an election, who . . . shall unlawfully accompany or follow any voter into a compartment, shall be deemed guilty of a misdemeanor, and subject to like fine and imprisonment, and shall be declared incapable of serving as an officer of election, or as agent or representative of a candidate at the polls, for three years from the date of the sentence.

. . . *Subsect.* 11–25. (Further penalties imposed for bribery, etc.)

. . . *Subsect.* 26. Irregularities or defects (*t*) in the mode of convening, holding, or conducting an election under this act shall constitute no defence to a prosecution for a violation of its provisions.

(*t*) S. Austr., § 71; Queens., § 85; Gt. Br., § 13; and NOTE 12, p. 64.

SECS. 21–28. (Miscellaneous provisions, corrupt practices, tribunals for contesting an election, etc.)

VII. NEW YORK.

AN ACT TO MORE FULLY SECURE THE INDEPENDENCE OF ELECTORS AND THE SECRECY OF THE BALLOT. (1888.) (a)

(a) For the differences between this act and the bill now pending, see Appendix I.

The people of the State of New York, represented in Senate and Assembly, do enact as follows:

SECTION 1. All ballots cast in elections for public officers within this State shall be printed and distributed at public expense, as hereinafter provided. The printing of ballots and cards of instruction for the electors in each county, and the delivery of the same to the election officers, as provided in Section 18 of this act, shall be a county charge, the payment of which shall be provided for in the same manner as the payment of other county expenses.

SECT. 2. Any convention, as hereinafter defined, held for the purpose of making nominations to public office, and also electors to the number hereinafter specified, may nominate candidates for public offices to be filled by election within the State. A convention, within the meaning of this act, is an organized assemblage of delegates representing a political party which at the last election before the holding of such convention polled at least three per cent of the entire vote cast in the State, county, or other division or district for which the nomination is made.

SECT. 3. All nominations made by any such convention shall be certified as follows: The certificate of nomination, which shall be in writing, shall contain the name of each person nominated, his residence, and the office for which he is nominated, and shall designate the party or principle which such convention represents. It shall be signed by the presiding officer and secretary of such convention, who shall add to their signatures their respective places of residence, and acknowledge the same before an officer duly authorized to take acknowledgments. A certificate of such acknowledgment shall be appended to said instrument.

SECT. 4. Certificates of nomination shall be filed with the Secretary of State (*a'*) for the nomination of candidates for offices to be filled by the electors of the entire State, or of any district or division of a greater extent than one county. For all other nominations to public offices, certificates of nomination shall be filed with the clerks (*a'*) of the respective counties wherein the offices are to be filled by the electors. The certificate of nomination for Assemblyman in the counties of Fulton and Hamilton shall be filed in the office of the County Clerk of Hamilton County, and a copy thereof certified by said County Clerk of Hamilton County shall be filed in the office of the County Clerk of Fulton County.

(*a'*) Mass., § 6; S. Austr., § 48; Queens., § 49; Gt. Br., B, § 8, D, § 1 (3); Belg., § 106; Ky., § 2.

SECT. 5. A candidate for public office may be nominated otherwise than by a convention in the manner following: A certificate of nomination containing the name of the candidate to be nominated, with the other information required to be given in the certificates provided for in Section 3 of this act, shall be signed by electors residing within the district or political division for which candidates are to be presented, equal in number (*b*) to at least one per cent of the entire vote cast at the last preceding election in the State, county, or other division or district for which the nomination is to be made, provided, however, that the number of signatures so required shall not exceed one thousand when the nomination is for an office to be filled by the electors of the entire State, and shall not exceed one hundred when the election is for an office to be filled by the electors of a county, district, or other division less than the State in extent, and provided also that the said signatures need not all be appended to one paper. Such a certificate, when made as above prescribed, may be filed as provided for in Section 4 of this act, with

(*b*) Mass., § 4; S. Austr., § 48; Queens., § 49; Gt. Br., A, § 1; Belg., §§ 106, 155; Ky., § 2; and NOTE 2, p. 53.

the same effect as a certificate of nomination made by a party convention.

SECT. 6. No certificate of nomination shall contain the name of more than one candidate for each office to be filled. No person shall join in nominating more than one nominee for each office to be filled ; and no person shall accept a nomination to more than one office.

SECT. 7. The Secretary of State shall cause to be preserved in his office all certificates of nomination filed therein under the provisions of this act, and each county clerk shall cause to be preserved in his office all certificates of nomination filed therein under the provisions of this act.

SECT. 8. Certificates of nomination, filed with the Secretary of State, shall be filed not more than sixty days and not less than twenty days (*c*) before the day fixed by the law for the election of the persons in nomination. Certificates of nomination herein directed to be filed with the clerk of the county shall be filed not more than sixty and not less than fifteen days (*c*) before election.

(*c*)
Mass., § 6;
S. Austr., § 46;
Queens., §§ 48, 49;
Gt. Br., B, §§ 4, 14, D, § 1 (3);
Belg., § 105;
Ky., § 2.

SECT. 9. Not less than eighteen days before an election to fill any public office, the Secretary of State shall certify to the County Clerk of each county within which any of the electors may by law vote for candidates for such office, the names and the description of each person nominated for such office, as specified in the certificates of nomination filed with the Secretary of State.

SECT. 10. At least seven days before an election to fill any public office, the County Clerk of each county shall cause to be published (*d*) in at least two newspapers within the county, the nominations to office certified to him by the Secretary of State, and also those filed with the County Clerk. He shall make not less than two such publications in each of such newspapers before election. One of such publications in each newspaper shall be upon the last day upon which such newspaper is issued before election. Such publication shall be made in two news-

(*d*)
Mass., §§ 14, 15;
S. Austr., § 50;
Queens., §§ 50, 53;
Gt. Br., B, § 9, D, § 1 (3);
Belg., § 112;
Ky., § 5.

papers, representing the political parties that at the last preceding election cast the largest and next largest number of votes; the list of nominations published by the county clerks of the respective counties shall be arranged, as far as practicable, in the order and form in which they will be printed upon the ballot.

SECT. 11. The Secretary of State shall not certify the name of a candidate whose certificate of nomination shall have been filed in his office, who shall have notified him in a writing signed and executed with the formalities prescribed for the execution of an instrument to entitle it to record, that he will not accept (e) the nomination contained in the certificate of nomination. The County Clerk shall not include in the publication to be made according to Section 10 hereof the name of any candidate whose certificate of nomination shall have been filed in his office who shall have notified him in like manner that he will not accept the nomination. The names of such candidates shall not be included in the names of the candidates to be printed in the ballots as hereinafter provided. *(e) Mass., § 8; Queens., § 54; Gt. Br., A, § 1, D, § 1 (7).*

SECT. 12. Whenever a proposed constitutional amendment or other question is to be submitted to the people of the State for popular vote, the Secretary of State shall duly, and not less than thirty days before election, certify the same to the clerk of each county of the State, and the clerk of each county shall include the same in the publication provided for in Section ten of this act.

SECT. 13. Except as in this act otherwise provided, it shall be the duty of the County Clerk of each county to provide printed ballots for every election for public officers in which electors or any of the electors within the county participate, and to cause to be printed in the appropriate ballot the name of every candidate whose name has been certified to, or filed with the County Clerk in the manner provided for in this act. Ballots, other than those printed by the respective county clerks according to the provisions of this act, shall not be cast or counted (f) in any election. Nothing in this act contained shall prevent any voter from *(f) See infra, § 23, note.*

writing upon his ballot (*g*) the name of any person for whom he desires to vote for any office, and such vote shall be counted the same as if printed upon the ballot.

(*g*)
Mass., § 10;
Ky., § 9; and
Note 16, p. 66.

SECT. 14. Except as otherwise provided in this act, every ballot printed as herein prescribed shall be printed in accordance with the existing provisions of law. All ballots shall contain the name of every candidate whose nomination for any office specified in the ballot has been certified to and filed according to the provisions of this act, and no other name. The names of candidates nominated by each party shall be grouped together (*h*) upon the proper ballot, and each group shall be headed by the name of the political party by which the candidates comprising said group were placed in nomination as described in the certificates of nomination. There shall be a margin on each side, at least half an inch wide, and a reasonable space between the names to be printed thereon, so that the voter may clearly indicate, in the way to be hereafter pointed out, the candidate or candidates for whom he wishes to cast his ballot.

(*h*)
Mass., § 10;
S. Austr., § 55;
Queens., § 58;
Gt. Br., B, § 22,
D, § 1 (6);
Belg., §§ 114, 115;
Ky., § 4, and
Note 4, p. 55.

SECT. 15. Whenever the Secretary of State has duly certified to any County Clerk any question to be submitted to a vote of the people, the County Clerk shall prepare and distribute ballots of such form as will enable the electors to vote upon the question in the manner hereinafter provided.

SECT. 16. The County Clerk of each county shall provide for each election district in the county one hundred ballots of each kind to be voted in the district, for every fifty or fraction of fifty electors (*i*) registered at the last preceding election in the district. If there is no registry in the district, the County Clerk shall provide ballots to the number of one hundred for every fifty or fraction of fifty electors who voted at the last election in the district.

(*i*)
Mass., § 12;
S. Austr. § 56;
Queens., § 58;
Ky., § 3.

SECT. 17. Whenever it shall appear by affidavit that an error or omission has occurred in the publication of the names or description of the candidates nominated for office, or in the printing of the ballots, the Supreme Court of the State may upon application by any elector, by order, require the County Clerk to correct such error, or to show cause why such error should not be corrected.

SECT. 18. Before the opening of the polls at any election of public officers within any county, the County Clerk of the county shall cause to be delivered to the board of inspectors of election of each election district which is within the county, and in which the election is to be held, at the polling-place of the district, the proper number of ballots of each kind to be used in the district.

SECT. 19. At the same time, and in the same manner, as inspectors of election are appointed or elected, two ballot clerks for each election district in the State shall be appointed or elected, whose duty it shall be to have charge of the ballots, and to furnish them to the voters in the manner hereinafter provided; such ballot clerks shall possess the same qualifications as inspectors of election. No elector shall vote for more than one person for said office of ballot clerk at the same time, and no political party shall nominate more than one person for that office. The two persons in each election district, when inspectors of election are elected, who shall receive the highest and next highest number of votes for the office, shall serve as such at all elections except town-meetings to be held therein during the ensuing year; whenever inspectors of election are not elected but appointed, such ballot clerks shall be appointed, and their appointment certified at the same time and in the same manner as is now provided for in the case of inspectors; but in making such appointments one of the ballot clerks in each election district shall be taken from the political party that polled the largest number of votes at the last preceding election, and the other from the party that polled the next largest number.

SECT. 20. Except in the City and County of New York, all officers upon whom is imposed by law the duty of designating polling-places shall provide in each polling-

(j)
Mass., § 21;
S. Austr. § 54;
Queens., § 59;
Gt. Br., B,
§ 16;
Belg., § 117;
Ky., § 8;
and Note 5, p. 58.

place designated by them (*j*) a sufficient number of places, booths, or compartments, which shall be furnished with such supplies and conveniences as shall enable the voter conveniently to prepare his ballot for voting and in which electors may mark their ballots, screened from observation, and a guard-rail so constructed that only persons within such rail can approach within five feet of the ballot-boxes or the places or compartments herein provided for. The number of such places or compartments shall not

(k)
Mass., § 21;
Queens., § 59;
Gt. Br., B,
§ 16;
Belg., § 118;
Ky., § 8.

be less than one for every seventy-five electors (*k*) who voted at the last preceding election in the district. No person other than electors engaged in receiving, preparing, or depositing their ballots shall be permitted to be within

(l)
Mass., § 21;
S. Austr., § 59;
Queens., § 59;
Gt. Br., B,
§ 21;
Belg., § 97;
Ky., § 17;
and Note 1, p. 52.

said rail (*l*) except by authority of the inspectors of elections. In the City and County of New York the Chief of the Bureau of Elections shall provide such places or compartments and guard-rails. The expense of providing such places or compartments and guard-rails shall be a public charge, and shall be provided for in each town and city in the same manner as the other election expenses. On or before the 1st day of January, 1889, and every year thereafter, the officers of the several cities and towns now charged by law with the division or alteration of election districts, shall as far as necessary, alter or divide the existing election districts in such a manner that each election district shall contain not more than three hundred voters; and such division or alteration shall take effect immediately. Except as in this section otherwise provided, such division or alteration shall be subject to the existing provisions of law.

(m)
Mass., § 22;
S. Austr., § 58, IV.;
Queens., § 71;
Gt. Br., B,
§ 50;
Belg., § 123;
Ky., § 7;
and Note 6, p. 59.

SECT. 21. On any day of election of public officers in any election district, each qualified elector shall be entitled to receive from the ballot clerks one ballot for each of the offices for which the elector desires to vote. It shall be the duty of such ballot clerks (*m*) to deliver such ballots to the elector. Before delivering any ballot to an elector the two ballot

(n)
Mass.,, § 10;
S. Austr., § 57;

clerks shall write their names or initials (*n*) upon the back of the ballot, immediately under the printed indorsement.

SECT. 22. On receipt of his ballots the elector shall forthwith, and without leaving the polling-place, retire alone to one of the places, booths, or compartments provided to prepare his ballots. He shall prepare his ballots by marking a cross (*o*) before or after the name of the person or persons for whom he intends to vote — thus, X ; or in case of a ballot containing a constitutional amendment or a question to be submitted to the vote of the people, by crossing out therefrom parts of the ballot in such a manner that the remaining part shall express his vote upon the question submitted. After preparing his ballots, the elector shall fold each of them so that the face of the ballot will be concealed, and so that the printed indorsement and the signatures and initials of the ballot-clerks thereon may be seen. He shall then vote forthwith and before leaving the polling-place.

Queens., § 71;
Gt. Br., A, § 2, B, § 24;
Belg. §§ 123, 151;
Ky., §§ 4, 7; and NOTE 7, p. 59.

(*o*)
Mass., § 23;
S. Austr., § 58, VI.;
Queens., § 73;
Gt. Br., A, § 2, B, § 25,
C. "Form of Directions for Voters,"
Belg., A, § 124, B, § 1;
Ky., § 9; and NOTE 9, p. 62.

Provided, however, that any elector who desires to vote for an entire group may mark a cross as above described before or after the political organization of such group (*o*), and shall then be deemed to have voted for all the persons named in such group.

SECT. 23. Not more than one person shall be permitted to occupy any one booth at one time; and no person shall remain in or occupy a booth longer than may be necessary to prepare his ballot, and in no event longer than five minutes (*p*).

SECT. 24. Any voter who shall by accident or mistake spoil his ballot (*q*) so that he cannot conveniently vote the same, may, on returning said spoiled ballot to the ballot clerks and satisfying them that such spoiling was not intentional, receive another in place thereof. Every elector who does not vote any ballot delivered to him, shall, before leaving the polling-place, return such ballot to the ballot clerks having charge of the ballots.

(*p*)
Mass., § 23;
Ky., § 12.

(*q*)
Mass., § 24;
S. Austr., § 58, VIII.;
Gt. Br., B, § 28;
Belg., § 125;
Ky., § 9.

SECT. 25. Any elector who declares under oath to the ballot clerks that he cannot read or write, or that by reason of physical disability he is unable to mark his ballots (*r*), may declare his choice of candidates to either

(*r*)
Mass., § 25;
S. Austr., § 58, VII.;

Queens., § 73;
Gt. Br., B, § 26;
Belg., § 123;
Ky., § 10;
and Note 8,
p. 61.

of the ballot clerks, who, in the presence of the elector, shall prepare the ballots for voting in the manner hereinbefore provided; or such elector, after making such oath, may require one of such ballot clerks to read to him the contents of the ballot, so that the elector can ascertain the relative position of the names of the candidates on each ballot, whereupon the elector shall retire to one of the places, booths, or compartments provided, to prepare his ballots in the manner hereinbefore provided.

SECT. 26. No inspector of election shall deposit any ballot upon which the names or initials of the ballot clerks as hereinbefore provided for does not appear.

SECT. 27. The County Clerk of each county shall cause to be printed in large type on cards in English and in such other languages as he deems necessary, instructions for the guidance of electors in preparing their ballots. He shall furnish twelve such cards, each printed in all the languages determined upon by him, to the board of inspectors of elections in each election district, at the same time and in the same manner as the printed ballots. The board of inspectors of elections shall post not less than one of such cards in each place or compartment provided for the preparation of ballots, and not less than three of such cards elsewhere in and about the polling-place upon the day of election. Said cards shall be printed in large, clear type, and shall contain full instructions to the voters as to what should be done, (1) to obtain ballots for voting; (2) to prepare the ballots for deposit in the ballot-boxes; (3) to obtain a new ballot in the place of one accidentally spoiled; also a copy of Sections 30 and 32 of this act.

(s)
Ante, § 13;
Mass., § 26;
S. Austr., § 64;
Queens., § 76;
Gt. Br., A, § 2;
Belg., §§ 124, 147;
Ky., § 11;
and Note 10,
p. 63.

SECT. 28. In the canvass of the votes, any ballot which is not endorsed by the names or initials of the ballot clerks, as provided in this act, shall be void and shall not be counted (s), and any ballot or parts of a ballot from which it is impossible to determine the elector's choice shall be void and shall not be counted (s). Such ballots shall be treated and preserved in the same manner as defective ballots.

SECT. 29. No person shall (1) falsely make, or fraudulently deface, or fraudulently destroy any certificate of nomination, or any part thereof; or (2) file any certificate of nomination knowing the same or any part thereof to be falsely made; or (3) suppress any certificate of nomination which has been duly filed, or any part thereof; or (4) forge or falsely make the official endorsement on any ballot. Every person violating any of the provisions of this section shall be deemed guilty of a felony.

SECT. 30. No person shall, during the election, remove or destroy any of the supplies or other conveniences placed in the booths as aforesaid for the purpose of enabling the voter to prepare his ballot. No person shall, during an election, remove, tear down, or deface, the cards printed for the instruction of voters. Every person wilfully violating any of the provisions of this section shall be deemed guilty of a misdemeanor.

SECT. 31. Every public officer upon whom any duty is imposed by this act, who shall wilfully neglect or omit to perform such duty (*t*), shall be deemed guilty of a misdemeanor; and upon conviction thereof shall be punished by imprisonment in the county jail or penitentiary for a term of not less than six months and not more than three years, or by a fine of not less than two hundred and fifty dollars, and not more than three thousand dollars, or by both such fine and imprisonment. (*t*) Mass., § 30; S. Austr., § 85. Queens., § 120; Gt. Br., A, § 11; and NOTE 11, p. 64.

SECT. 32. No officer of election shall disclose to any person the name of any candidate for whom any elector has voted. No officer of election shall do any electioneering on election day. No person whatever shall do any electioneering on election day within any polling-place, or within one hundred feet of any polling-place. No person shall remove any ballot from any polling-place before the closing of polls. No person shall apply for or receive any ballot in any polling-place other than that in which he is entitled to vote. No person shall show his ballot after it is marked to any person in such a way as to reveal the contents thereof or the name of the candidate or candidates for whom he has marked his vote, nor shall any person (except an inspector of election) receive, from any voter, a ballot prepared by him for voting, or examine such ballot, or solicit the voter to show the same. No person shall ask another at a polling-place for whom he intends to vote. No voter shall receive a ballot from any other person than one of the ballot clerks, nor shall any person other than a ballot clerk deliver a ballot to such voter. No voter shall deliver any ballot to the inspectors to be voted except such as he has received from a ballot clerk. No voter shall place any mark upon his ballot by which it may be afterward identified as the one voted by him. Whoever shall violate any provision of this section shall be deemed guilty of a misdemeanor.

SECT. 33. All the provisions of this act relating to County Clerks shall apply in the City and County of New York to the Chief of the Bureau of Elections, and not to the County Clerk. Such provisions shall apply in the City of Brooklyn to the Board of Elections, and not to the County Clerk of Kings County.

SECT. 34. This act shall not apply to elections for town and village officers in towns and villages where there is no provision by law for the registration of electors, nor to elections for public officers determined otherwise than by ballot.

SECT. 35. All acts and parts of acts inconsistent with the provisions of this act are hereby repealed.

SECT. 36. This act shall take effect January one, eighteen hundred and eighty-nine.[1]

[1] It was vetoed by the Governor.

VIII.

THE AUSTRALIAN BALLOT SYSTEM AS EMBODIED IN THE STATUTES OF TASMANIA, NEW ZEALAND, NEW SOUTH WALES, VICTORIA, WEST AUSTRALIA, THE DOMINION OF CANADA, THE PROVINCES OF ONTARIO AND OF QUEBEC, WISCONSIN, THE GRAND DUCHY OF LUXEMBOURG, ITALY, NORWAY, ETC.

A. TASMANIA.

Parliamentary Elections Act, 1858 (21 Vict. No. 32).

The following are the special features of the Tasmanian legislation : —

By § 62, any two electors may nominate a candidate.

By § 61, the ballots are required to be signed or stamped on the back by the Clerk of the Peace, who distributes them to the various Returning Officers; and upon their receipt by the latter they are again stamped or countersigned before being distributed to voters.

By § 69, the voter is required to express his vote by striking out the names of all candidates other than those for whom he intends to vote.

By § 71, provision is made for rendering assistance, in marking the ballot, to those only who are blind.

In other respects no notable variation is found in the system in use in Tasmania. In the Rural Municipalities Act, 1865 (29 Vict. No. 8), the parliamentary provisions are adopted without material difference.

B. New Zealand.

Regulation of Elections Act, 1881 (45 Vict. No. 12).

This Act, applying only to elections for Representatives to the General Assembly, supersedes, for such elections, the Regulation of Elections Act, 1870 (33–34 Vict. No. 18), which, for the election of members of the Provincial Councils and of Provincial Superintendents, apparently is still in force. The later Act makes several changes, evidently intended as improvements called for by experience. The provisions to be noticed are as follows:—

By § 12, a candidate must be proposed by one elector, and seconded by another.

By § 30, the method of identifying the official ballot is to be as follows: the Returning Officer writes upon the back of the ballot his initials, and upon the lower left-hand corner of the ballot, on the back, the registered number of the voter, and "after securing the said corner by gum or otherwise," stamps upon it the official mark.

The original method employed in the earlier Act consisted in stamping the official mark on the back of the ballot, and placing near the lower edge, on the back, the registered number of the voter or some other identifying mark. Secrecy was provided for by forbidding the examination of the backs of ballots while counting; but apparently this regulation had failed to attain its object.

By § 33, "if any voter desires it, the Returning Officer, and, if necessary, an interpreter," are to retire to one of the compartments with the voter, and mark the ballot according to his instructions.

Under the earlier Act, the corresponding provision limited the right to give such assistance to the specific cases of blindness and inability to read.

By § 32, the vote is to be expressed by striking out the names of candidates not voted for.

C. Victoria.

Electoral Act, 1865 (No. 279).

The important variations of the Victorian system are as follows: —

Nomination-papers are to be signed by ten electors. As in Queensland, a deposit — £50 or £100, according to the office — is required at the time of nomination, to be returned if the candidate withdraws or receives one-fifth of the number of votes received by the successful candidate. The period between the days of nomination and election is to be from 3 to 14 days.

The vote is expressed by striking out from the list of names all except those for whom the vote is cast. The method of identifying the official ballot is to place upon the ballot, before the voting begins, the signature or the initials of the Returning Officer; the registered number of the voter is also placed on the back of the ballot, and the officers are forbidden, in counting, to examine the back of the ballot.

D. New South Wales.

Elections Act, 1880 (44 Vict. No. 13); *Municipalities Act*, 1867 (31 Vict. No. 12).

The editor has not been able to obtain a copy of these statutes for examination, and cannot state their provisions in detail. They follow, however, the general plan of the kindred Australian statutes. Nominations (in municipal elections) must be handed in 7 days at least before the day of election; the ballots must be signed by the poll-clerk; and the vote is expressed by striking out the names of candidates not voted for.

E. West Australia.

Ballot Act, 1877 (41 Vict. No. 15).

This Act applies only to elections for the Legislature. The provisions to be noted are as follows: —

By § 4, a nomination-paper is required to contain the names of 6 electors, and to be accompanied by a deposit of £25, returnable as provided in the Queensland Act, *ante*.

By § 5, II., the ballot is to have a counterfoil attached, and a number is written or printed on the back of the ballot, the same number being written or printed on the face of the counterfoil.

By § 9, the vote is required to be expressed "by making a cross or other mark" within the square opposite the name. In the "Directions to Voters," however, the direction declares absolutely that the voter "will place a cross," etc.

By § 9, the Returning Officer's initials are to be placed on the back of the ballot before delivery to the voter, and the voter's name is to be written on the counterfoil.

By § 14, the Returning Officer is to reject, at the counting, any ballot "on which is written any matter or thing which is not justified by this Act to be written thereon," or in which votes are cast for more candidates than are to be voted for. In the "Directions for Voters," it is also stated (though no section of the Act appears to authorize it) that "any mark by which the voter may be afterwards identified" will invalidate the ballot.

There is no provision authorizing assistance to be rendered to any class of voters.

F. DOMINION OF CANADA.

Dominion Elections Act, 1874 (37 Vict. c. 9), as amended by 41 Vict. c. 6 (1878).

The important provisions to be noticed in this Act, which is one of the best conceived among the various statutes dealing with the subject, are as follows: —

By § 18, any 25 electors may nominate a candidate.

By § 19, the nomination-paper must contain the consent in writing of the person nominated, unless he is absent from the Province in which the election is to be held.

By § 19, the sum of 50 dollars must be paid to the Returning Officer at the time of handing in the nomination-paper.

By § 43, and by § 3 of the amending Act, the ballot-paper is to have a detachable counterfoil, as shown by Form (1), *infra*, with the counterfoil attached. At the time of delivering the ballot to the intending voter, the Returning Officer places his initials upon the back of the ballot, and the registered number of the voter upon the counterfoil. When the ballot has been marked by the voter, and is presented for deposit in the ballot-box, the Returning Officer, by noting his initials upon the back of the ballot, and the number upon the counterfoil, is enabled to identify the ballot as an official one, and also to know that the ballot is presented by the same voter to whom it was originally given out. Before the ballot is deposited, the officer detaches and destroys the counterfoil.

It is to be noted that, by § 2 of the amending Act, the use of an envelope, in which, by § 43 of the original Act, the ballot was required to be placed, is abandoned.

By § 6 of the amending Act, the voter is to "mark his ballot, marking a cross with a pencil on any part of the ballot-paper within the division containing the name of the candidate for whom he intends to vote." In the original Act (§ 45), the method was to mark "a cross on the right-hand side opposite the name of" the desired candidate. But to obviate the possibility of the irregular methods of marking which voters were found now and then to employ, the margin on the left of the names and the upright dividing line on the right were discarded, and the ballot was printed in the shape shown in Form (1), *infra*, probably the best form now in use. This led to the change in the wording of § 45 of the original Act.

By § 48, official assistance may be rendered to voters "unable to read, or incapacitated by blindness or other physical cause" from voting in the prescribed manner.

By § 55, the void ballots are to include, besides those containing votes for more candidates than are to be elected, all ballots "not similar to those supplied by the Deputy Returning Officer," and all those upon which there is any writing or mark " by which the voter could be identified."

By § 80, it is provided, as in the English statute, that no informality shall vitiate the election, if the principles of the Act have been followed, and if the result of the election has not been affected.

FORM 1. *Ballot-Paper.*

ELECTION FOR THE ELECTORAL DISTRICT OF	, 18 .

	DOE.
I.	JOHN DOE, Township of Nepean, County of Carleton, Yeoman.

	ROE.
II.	RICHARD ROE, of the town of Prescott, County of Grenville, Merchant.

	STILES.
III.	GEOFFREY STILES, of 10 Sparks St., Ottawa, Physician.

	STILES.
IV.	JOHN STILES, of 3 Elgin St., Ottawa, Barrister-at-Law.

(Counterfoil.)

G. QUEBEC.

Quebec Elections Act, 1875 (38 Vict. c. 7), as amended by 39 Vict. c. 13 (1875) and 46 Vict. c. 2 (1883).

The points essential to be noticed are :—

By § 105, a candidate may be nominated by 25 electors.

By § 106, the candidate's consent in writing is necessary unless he is absent.

By § 166, the identification of the ballot is secured by requirements as to initials, counterfoils, etc., similar to the requirements of the Dominion Act (1878) already described. The Quebec Act (1875) was, in fact, the earlier of the two, and apparently inspired the Dominion amendment of 1878. Its details, however, are different and better in this respect: the counterfoil, or "annex," as it is called, is printed upon the back of the ballot (see Form (2), *infra*), so that in the operation of verifying and detaching the annex, the back of the ballot is presented to the officer, and its face is not liable to be exposed to view.

By § 170, the voter is to " mark his ballot-paper, marking a cross or other mark on the right-hand side, opposite the name of" the desired candidate. But by § 17 of the amending Act of 1875, the words "or other mark" were omitted, and a pencil was required to be used.

By § 190, the validity of ballots is to be determined by rules similar to those of the Dominion Act.

By § 222, a provision similar to that of the English Act declares that mere informalities shall not invalidate the election.

FORM 2. *Ballot-Paper.*

Election for Electoral District of , 18 .	1	DUREAU. (JEAN DUREAU, town of Sorel, County of Richelieu, Merchant.)
	2	MEUNIER. (JOSEPH MEUNIER, city of Montreal, 10 Fontaine St., Montreal.)
	3	RICHARD. (ANTOINE RICHARD, of the parish of St. Henri, County of Lévis, Farmer.)
	4	RICHARD. (JOSEPH RICHARD, of the town and county of Lévis, Advocate.)

[Over.]

Reverse of Form 2.

H. Ontario.

Elections (*Act* Ontario Revised Statutes, 1887, c. 9).

The Ballot Act of Great Britain is followed in substance, but the following provisions may be noted: —

By § 48, a nomination may be made by a single elector, and if at the time and place of nomination a poll is demanded by any elector, it is to be granted.

By § 63 (3), " the numbers and names of every candidate shall, if practicable, be distinctly printed in ink of different colors," the candidates selecting the colors on the day of nomination, or the Returning Officer assigning them in case of disagreement.

By § 90 (7), the English method of identifying the ballot is in substance adopted; a number is previously stamped on the back of the ballot and on the face of the counterfoil; the voter's registered number is placed on the counterfoil at the time of delivering the ballot, and the officer's name or initials are stamped or signed (signed only, by the original Act of 1874, c. 5) on the back of the ballot and on the counterfoil.

By § 91, the vote is to be expressed " by placing a cross thus ✕ on the right-hand side, opposite the name of the candidate for whom he desires to vote, *or at any other place within the division which contains the name of such candidate.*" The words in italics were for the first time inserted in the revision of 1887. They are intended, however, not to change the method of marking (for the " Directions to Voters " still require the mark to be "at the right-hand side " only), but to save the votes of those whose mark is not formally made.

The provisions of the Municipal Act (Rev. Stat. 1887, c. 184), applying the same system to municipal elections, are substantially the same as those of the Elections Act, except that in the ballot the use of counterfoils and of colors is discarded. A form of the ballot used in municipal elections is given below as Form (3).

By § 205, no mere informality is to vitiate the election (as in the English Act).

FORM 3. *Ballot-Paper.*

Election for Members of the Municipal Council of the Village [or Township] of _____, in the County of _____, Polling Subdivision No. _____ day of January, 18__ .		
For Reeve.	**BROWN.** (JOHN BROWN, of the village of Weston, Merchant.)	
	ROBINSON. (GEORGE ROBINSON, of the village of Weston, Physician.)	
For Deputy Reeve.	**ARMOUR.** (JACOB ARMOUR, of the village of Weston, Pumpmaker.)	
	BOYD. (ZACHARY BOYD, of the village of Weston, Tinsmith.)	
For Councillors.	**BULL.** (JOHN BULL, of the village of Weston, Butcher.)	
	JONES. (MORGAN JONES, of the village of Weston, Grocer.)	
	McALLISTER. (ALLISTER MCALLISTER, of the village of Weston, Tailor.)	
	O'CONNELL. (PATRICK O'CONNELL, of the village of Weston, Milkman.)	

I. Wisconsin.

Laws of 1887, *ch.* 350.

By § 1, each voting precinct is to be provided with two adjoining rooms, a "ticket room" and an "inspectors' and voting room." In the ticket room are to be tables or compartments, on or in which the tickets "prepared for the use of voters by any political party" are to be kept, "each class or kind being placed and kept in a separate compartment or upon a separate table," and a notice being placed over each class stating "the name or title by which the tickets are respectively classified or generally known." "Any chairman of a ward committee, or other person authorized by the ward committee of each political party," may deliver the proper tickets to the inspectors of election, who are to arrange them on the tables. "Every voter when in the ticket room shall be at liberty to select from the ballots kept there such as he may wish, taking one of each kind if he pleases."

For each table a custodian of tickets is to be appointed by the ward committee issuing the ticket. The custodians are to take an oath of office, and while inside the ticket room are not to "directly or indirectly solicit, request, or attempt to influence any voter" in respect to his vote. The custodians are to be paid the same fees as the clerks of election. A challenger is also appointed by each ward committee, and remains "in such convenient place to be designated by the inspectors," but outside the voting room, to challenge suspected votes. No undue advantage is to be given to any one of the challengers or custodians over his fellows.

The voter is admitted into the ticket room, where he selects his ticket or tickets. Only one voter at a time is to be admitted, and none others than the custodians and a single voter shall be permitted to remain in the room. At the door between the two rooms is to be one police officer, and at the outer door of the ticket room is to be another.

The voter passes into the voting room, casts his ballot, and passes out through another door.

No crowd is to be allowed within one hundred feet of either room during the election. No one shall solicit votes or offer tickets within the same limits. The mutilation, destruction, and theft of tickets is forbidden, as well as all attempts to solicit or influence voters while within either room. A penalty is also imposed upon those who request or receive anything of value from a candidate for services rendered or to be rendered in or about any election.

By § 2 the act is applied to all judicial and city elections (except special elections).[1]

J. LUXEMBOURG.

Consolidated Election Act of March 5, 1884.[*]

(*) Annuaire de lég. étrang., 1879 (vol. ix.), p. 592; 1884 (vol. xiv.), p. 527.

This act unites into one the previous statutes relating to elections, embodying and superseding the act of May 28, 1879, relating to legislative elections, and for the first time applying the same system to municipal elections. In most respects the Belgian law is followed and adopted, with certain simplifications suitable for the smaller constituencies of Luxembourg.

In legislative elections, nomination-papers are to be signed by five times as many electors as there are members to be elected, but in no case by less than ten. In

---

[1] The above act, while pointing in the direction of reform, has not established the two essential principles of improvement: (1) complete and compulsory secrecy in voting; (2) a single ballot containing all the names printed and distributed by the state. Its provisions will doubtless abolish disorder and tumult at the polls, and intimidation by brute force; but it is as easy as before to ascertain which way a vote is cast, and thus very little is gained toward relieving the electors from other and equally effective means of control; moreover, a bribe-taker can still prove his vote. Finally, the evils of the present nomination system do not seem to be reached; and several custodians of tickets at each precinct are added to the ranks of those who draw official pay for election services, and whose places add to the patronage under the control of local politicians.

municipal elections, the signatures of fifteen electors are necessary in the city of Luxembourg; of five electors in towns of more than three thousand inhabitants; and in other towns, of three electors, among whom may be the candidates themselves. The voter is directed to mark a cross, and the ballot is to be folded square. Every ballot folded differently, or containing any mark that could identify it, or containing a name other than those upon the official list, or more names than there are members to be elected, is void.

K. ITALY.

Acts of Jan. 22 and May 7, 1882, published in one by royal decree of Sept. 24, 1882.*   (*) Ann. de lég. étrang., 1882 (vol. xii.), p. 503.

The material provisions are as follows: —

TITLE III.

ART. 54. The election room shall be divided into two parts by a railing a metre or more in height, with an opening for passage from one part to the other. The voters shall remain during the voting in the outer portion; in the other shall sit the election officers. The table of the officers shall be so placed that at the close of the voting the electors may surround it. The tables at which the ballots are to be filled out shall be isolated, and so placed as to insure secrecy in voting.

ART. 59. The capital town of the district shall supply to the presiding election officers of the polling-places a municipal seal and a number of ballots of white (*a*) paper not less in number than the number of voters on the list of the polling-place. The use of any other ballots is forbidden. . . .   (*a*) Until this time the official ballot-paper had been blue.

ART. 63. As soon as the organization of the election officers has been recorded in the minutes of the proceedings, the name of one of the inspectors shall be drawn by lot, who shall sign on the back as many ballots as there are electors in the polling-district. As each ballot is signed, the presiding officer shall impress thereon the municipal seal referred to in art. 57, and shall place it in an urn of transparent glass. If the said inspector absents himself from the room, he shall sign no more ballots, and shall be replaced by another inspector similarly drawn by lot. The minutes shall record the names of the inspectors who sign the ballots and the number signed by each one.

ART. 64. The presiding officer shall cause each elector to be called in the order of his name on the list, and, after identifying him, shall draw a ballot from the urn and deliver it to him unfolded.

ART. 65. The elector who is called shall seat himself at one of the tables used for the purpose, and on the ballot which has been delivered to him shall write the names of the deputies for whom he wishes to vote. If the elector was a qualified voter before the passage of the present law but is unable to read and write (*b*), or if, through physical incapacity, known by or proved to the election officers, he cannot write his ballot, he shall be allowed to have it written by another elector selected by himself.

ART. 66. When the ballot is written, the voter shall deliver it folded to the presiding officer, who shall drop it into a second urn of transparent glass, placed on the table and visible to all. . . .

ART. 69. Ballots shall not be counted which are without the signature and seal required by art. 63, or which contain anything that identifies or is intended to identify the voter.

(*b*) By this act, which embraces all matters relating to the elective franchise, one of the suffrage qualifications is the ability to read and write.

L. NORWAY.

Act of July 1, 1884,* *amending the Electoral Act of* 1828.

(*) Ann. de lég. étrang., 1884 (vol. xiv.), p. 624.

ART. 2. . . . The electors shall be called in the order in which their names occur on the register. When the entire list has been called those who have not answered shall be called again; whoever is not then present will lose his vote.

ART. 3. . . . The presiding officer or some other election officer, shall deliver to each elector, when called, an envelope marked with the official seal, and shall direct him to a secluded place in the polling-station, where, without being seen by any one, he shall place his ballot in the envelope, a sufficient time being allowed for the purpose, and shall then drop it into an urn placed on the election table.

Art. 4. The envelopes used shall be of the same size, form, and color, and not transparent. The election officers shall see, at the time the envelopes are dropped into the urn, that they bear no mark on the outside. The ballots placed in the envelopes shall be of white paper, without signature or mark appended. If an envelope or ballot does not fulfil the requirements of this act, the ballot shall be thrown out as void. If several ballots are found in one envelope, they shall all be void.

M.

Austria.

By the law of April 2, 1873, at Austrian elections an official ballot paper is furnished the elector by the officers of election at the time of voting, and the voter retires to a secluded place and writes upon his ballot the name of the preferred candidate.[1] The editor is not aware that this provision is modelled upon the Australian method, and has no further information in detail as to the polling arrangements or other regulations.

N.

Other Countries.

In several states certain features of electoral procedure are parallel to provisions of the Australian system, and merit a brief notice.

In Hungary[2] nominations are open, and must be handed

---

[1] Charbonnier, " Organisation électorale de tous les pays civilisés," p. 153.

[2] Charbonnier, p. 180.

in to the officer of election at least half an hour before the opening of the polls. The vote, however, is not secret.

In France intending candidates are required to register themselves as such by taking the candidate's oath (*prêter serment*) before the proper officer a certain number of days previous to the election. The purpose of this, however, in no respect resembles the principle of the Australian system. The ballot in France is not an official one, containing the names of all candidates, but, as in this country, separate ballots are prepared by each party or candidate, and the oath-taking is a mere necessary form. Sir Charles Dilke relates[1] that it was a common joke in Paris to say, when departing in some direction, "I am on my way to my café, and am going to take the oath as a candidate."

In Greece, the objects of the Australian system are attained by provisions materially different in form, but so similar in effect that they deserve description.[2]

Nominations must be in writing signed by twelve electors (a much larger number, generally one twentieth of the electorate, but varying with the number of members to be elected, were formerly required), and delivered to the officer of elections at least twenty-five days previous to the election. A deposit of two hundred drachmas (about $40) is also required from each candidate. The voting is by means of balls. In the polling-place are arranged in a row ballot-boxes equal in number to the number of candidates, and on each is the name of a candidate, in plain letters. The right-hand half of the box is white with the word "Yes" upon the front: the left-hand half is black, with the word "No" upon it. Within are two bags, one placed to the right and the other to the left, with a partition between the two. A funnel, about ten inches long and five inches in diameter, projects at a slight upward angle from the front of the

---

[1] Parl. Papers, 1868-9, vol. viii., p. 402.

[2] See Charbonnier, p. 366; Parl. Papers, *ubi supra*, Test. of Arthur Arnold, p. 416.

box. After the voter has given his name and proved his right to vote he approaches the line of boxes. An election officer attends him from box to box, at each one giving him a small metal ball. The voter holds this up between the thumb and forefinger, to show that he has only a single ball, and thrusting his arm in the funnel drops his ball to the right or left according as he votes for or against the candidate, the movement of his hand of course being completely invisible. This he does at each box. At the close of the election the votes cast against each candidate are subtracted from the votes cast for him, and his total number is thus ascertained.

A little reflection will show that this system is by no means an inefficient one, and is capable of attaining very good results. But it is of course not adapted to a numerous electorate nor to communities whose traditions have not accustomed them to similar methods.[1]

[1] The Grecian system would seem to be a development of the old method of reckoning by tallies. In Hungary, until not many years ago, the electors voted with long, slender sticks, colored to represent the different candidates.

APPENDIX.

I.

The main points in which the New York bill of 1889, as reported by the committee, differs from the act of 1888, are as follows: —

In section 2, the privilege of making nominations is extended to "primary meetings;" and the political party which may nominate by convention or caucus need have obtained only one per cent of the entire vote cast.

In section 5, the maximum number of signatures necessary for a nomination to a state office is reduced to five hundred, and for a nomination in a lesser district to fifty. Each signer is also required to append his residence, occupation, and place of business, and to make oath to his signature and statements.

In section 8, the earliest day for filing nominations is changed from sixty to forty and thirty days, respectively, before election.

In section 13, provision for filling vacancies is made, as follows: —

"Section 13. Should any person so nominated die before election day, or decline the nomination as in this act provided, or should any certificate of nomination be insufficient or inoperative, the vacancy or vacancies thus occasioned may be filled in the manner required for original nominations. If the original nomination was made by a party convention which had delegated to a committee the power to fill vacancies, such committee may upon the occurring of such vacancies proceed to fill the same. The Chairman and Secretary of such committee shall thereupon make and file with the proper officer a certificate setting forth the cause of the vacancy, the name of the person nominated, the office for which he was nominated, the name of the person for whom the new nominee is to be substituted, the fact that the committee was authorized to fill vacancies, and such further information as is required to be given in an original certificate of nomination. The certificate so made shall be executed, acknowledged, and sworn to in the manner prescribed for the original certificate of nomination, and shall upon being filed at least eight days before election have the same force and effect as an original certificate of nomination. When such certificate shall be filed with the Secretary of State he shall in certifying the nominations to the various county clerks insert the name of the person who has thus been nominated to fill a vacancy in place of that of the original nominee. And in the event that he has already sent forward his certificate he shall forthwith certify to the clerks of the proper counties the name and description of the person so nominated to fill a vacancy, the office he is nominated for, the party or political principle he represents, and the name of the person for whom such nominee is substituted."

In section 15, the following provision is inserted: "Nothing in this act contained shall prevent any voter from writing or pasting upon his ballot the name of any person for whom he desires to vote for any office, and such vote shall be counted the same as if printed upon the ballot and marked by the voter, and any voter may take with him into the polling-place any printed or written memorandum or paper to assist him in marking or preparing his ballot, except as hereinafter otherwise provided."

In section 18, the number of ballots to be printed is changed to two hundred for every fifty electors.

In section 22, compartments are to be provided to the number of not less than one for every fifty electors. The clause "except by authority of the inspectors of elections" is struck out.

In section 24, "thus," in line 6, is changed to "for example." The following provision is inserted for the benefit of illiterates: "In marking such a ballot any elector shall be at liberty to use or copy any unofficial sample ballot which he may choose to mark or to have had marked in advance of entering the polling-place or booth, to assist him in marking the official ballot, but no elector shall be at liberty to use or bring into the polling-place any unofficial sample ballot printed upon paper of the color and quality now required to be used for the printing of ballots under the general election laws of this State." At the end of the section is added: "whose names shall not have been erased."

In section 25, the maximum time is changed to ten minutes, "provided the other booths or compartments are occupied."

Section 26 reads as follows (apparently for the purpose of avoiding Governor Hill's objection that the power to determine whether a ballot had been intentionally spoiled should not be left to the ballot clerk) : —

"SECTION 26. Any voter, who shall by accident or mistake spoil his ballot may, on returning said spoiled ballot, receive another in place thereof."

Section 27 obviates another of Governor Hill's objections by omitting the clause compelling illiterates to declare their votes to one of the officers, and by allowing persons physically disabled to take a friend into the compartment to mark for them. Illiterates are supposed to take advantage of section 24, *ante*, p. 154.

In section 30, the words "names or initials" are altered to "signature or autograph initials."

In section 34, the word "voter" is throughout very properly changed to "elector."

www.ingramcontent.com/pod-product-compliance
Lightning Source LLC
Chambersburg PA
CBHW030259170426
43202CB00009B/805